Elizabeth Marshall
181 Amaral Street
East Providence, RI 02915

BLUEBIRDS

NB

NATURE BOOKS PUBLISHERS

BLUEBIRDS

THEIR DAILY LIVES
AND
HOW TO ATTRACT
AND RAISE BLUEBIRDS

TINA AND CURTIS DEW
and
R.B. (REBER) LAYTON

NATURE BOOKS PUBLISHERS
JACKSON, MISSISSIPPI

All rights reserved

Copyright© 1986 by R.B. Layton

No part of this book may be reproduced or used in any form or by any means, electronic or mechanical, including photocopying and recording, or by any information storage and retrieval system, without permission in writing from the publisher. The only exception to this prohibition is for a reviewer who wishes to quote brief passages in connection with a review written for inclusion in a newspaper or magazine. For further information contact the publishers.

Manufactured in the United States of America

Mailing address:

NATURE BOOKS PUBLISHERS
Post Office Box 12157
Jackson, Mississippi 39236-2157
(601) 956-5686

First Printing 1986

Library of Congress
Cataloguing-in-Publication Data

Dew, Tina, 1956-
  Bluebirds: Their daily lives and how to attract and raise bluebirds.

  Bibliography: p.
  Includes index.
1. Bluebirds. 2. Birds, Attracting of I. Dew, Curtis, 1955- .II. Layton, Reber Boyce, 1912-
III. Title.
QL696.P255D48 1986   598.8'42   86-70315
ISBN 0-912542-06-3

To Dr. Lawrence Zeleny

The individual who is most responsible for alerting America to the near demise of the bluebird is Dr. Lawrence Zeleny. Early did he see the diminishing population of this lovely bird and come to its rescue.

Through his efforts, and of those around him whom he motivated, grew the organization of the North American Bluebird Society, with Dr. Zeleny as its founder. He is, indeed, a major missionary of the active bluebird conservation movement that is rapidly spreading across our continent.

Larry Zeleny has spent seventy continuous years working to aid bluebirds. He monitors his bluebird trail of sixty-five bluebird boxes every week during bluebird nesting season in Beltville, Maryland, his home. In addition, he finds time to actively assist in the volunteer help necessary to keep the North American Bluebird Society a leader in the bluebird conservation movement.

For his faithfulness to his favorite bird, the bluebird, this book is hereby dedicated.

Preface

This book is based upon actual experiences with bluebirds, what they do from month to month throughout the year. All three authors maintain active bluebird trails, monitored weekly, and producing over 300 new bluebirds each year.

Personal unsolicited letters about the daily lives of their bluebirds, written by Tina and Curtis Dew to their friends, R. B. (Reber) and Gray Layton, reveal more about the daily happenings in the bluebird world than can be found in any publications. Their letters were the inspiration for the writing of this book.

Upon receiving the first few letters from the Dews, the Laytons saw in them an example of unusual dedication to the bluebird cause that needed to be shared with others. The letters were written in such a spirit of loyalty to their bluebirds that the Laytons immediately wrote back and urged Tina and Curtis to keep writing them about their bluebirds. No mention was made of the desire to publish the letters. Only after receiving letters to cover a complete year cycle did the Laytons visit the Dews, reveal their desire to publish the letters, and persuade them to permit their publication.

No attempt was made to edit the letters into a scientific treatise on the bluebird. Instead, the nomenclature was kept in layman's language. Male and female bluebirds, referred to as "he" and "she". "Mr. Blue", and "Mrs. Blue", etc. were left intact for better enjoyment of the bluebird message that the Dews were telling so well.

The personal flavor of the letters adds to their interest. From the Dew letters the reader will gain an insight into the art of bluebirding to such an extent that he, too, may become as dedicated to the cause as Tina and Curtis.

In addition to the letters, co-author Layton has provided basic information on ways to attract and raise bluebirds, where to find birding supplies, recommended birding journals, a select annotated bibliography of bird books, and a large Q. and A. section about bluebirds.

With these combined presentations the reader will find a complete account of bluebirding at its best.

The authors and publishers acknowledge with thanks the permission to use information from their publications: The North American Bluebird Society; Joanne K. Solem, editor of *Sialia*; the United States Fish and Wildlife Service; and the United States Department of Agriculture. Credits are respectfully given at appropriate places within the text. They also wish to give special thanks to Gray Layton for her valuable assistance with every aspect of the book.

Cover Photo by CURTIS DEW
BLUEBIRD TAKING HIS MORNING EXERCISE

CONTENTS

THE DAILY LIVES OF BLUEBIRDS

by
Tina and Curtis Dew

*A twelve month diary of observations
told in letters*

and
HOW TO ATTRACT AND RAISE BLUEBIRDS

by
R.B. (Reber) Layton

November 28

Dear G. and R.

Curtis and I really enjoyed your letter last month. I understand your delay in writing; I am sorry I haven't written you back any sooner. I just seem to get behind in all my correspondence. I am afraid I am guilty of using all my free time at home to bird watch and at work lately we've been very busy and I haven't had a chance to write. When home I've been guilty of grabbing something to read instead of catching up on my letter writing. I love to read about birds and I guess that we subscribe to too many nature magazines, *Sialia*, *Nature Society News*, *Audubon*, *Living Bird Quarterly*, etc.

Our bluebirds are doing great! We had seventy-seven babies to fledge this past summer. We are putting up about twenty more houses in a couple of weeks. That will give us fifty. We would have them up already except we couldn't dig holes in the ground for the posts. The ground was like concrete, but, now, since it has rained, the ground is moist and we plan to get the posts in the ground real soon because the bluebirds do love perching on the houses and playing in and out of them, even though it's getting to be winter time. We checked our existing trail last August and at that time we cleaned out all of the houses well. We checked them again last week and at least six of them had small nests with about one-half to one inch of straw inside and half of the others had sprigs of straw in them. The young bluebirds had been playing and practicing nest building. We've observed that the young birds do this a lot in early winter and early spring.

We have about eight bluebirds that sleep in our yard and eat raisins on a regular basis. We get up at 5:15 every morning to eat breakfast and dress before the bluebirds get up. We put some raisins out on the feeder bench in the front yard and sit on the front porch about twenty feet away and watch the bluebirds drop down and eat their raisins at daybreak. No matter how cold it is, we bundle up to watch them, even though we can see them from inside. We like being outside so we can hear their little sounds. After about fifteen minutes of sitting around on the fence and eating raisins, they go on their way to different woods and fields to find bugs, but they are home several times during the day to go in one of the raisin feeders, or drink and bathe in one of the bird baths.

I just have to tell you what they did last week. It was Wednesday, the day we had a big rain and windstorm. We happened to get off work early and I got home earlier than usual, about 3:00 p.m. - we regularly get home at four thirty. When we reach home, the bluebirds usually are up in the trees ready and waiting for food. Well, today after we pulled in the carport, three baby bluebirds flew up on the power line and were fussing at us. That was unusual, because they don't normally come flying up as soon as our car pulls into the garage. I watched them a minute or two and then took my groceries inside. When I got inside the house, I noticed that the front bluebird feeder was missing. The windstorm had blown it off its post. It had landed about twenty feet from the post, and miraculously neither piece of the glass was broken. I called Curtis and he put the feeder back up and put some new raisins in it. Our other bluebird feeder in the back yard was empty of food. The bluebirds had already eaten up their daily supply of raisins. Anyhow, Curtis put the front feeder back up and put a new supply of raisins in it and those three baby bluebirds came up and went in the feeder and ate two raisins apiece in less than two minutes after Curtis put the feeder back up. They amuse us so much!

I really love our bluebirds! No matter where we go walking on the farm we see bluebirds. I wish they'd all stay in the yard so we could watch them. Our couple that raised all the babies in the yard are still pretty territorial. They still fight off other bluebirds regularly.

We went to the Mississippi Ornithological Society meeting at Tishomingo State Park last month. It was the first meeting we'd ever attended and we really enjoyed it. We met lots of new nice people, several from the Jackson Audubon Society. Larry Gates, president of the Mississippi Ornithological Society, and his wife, Terry, were so cordial.

They live in Hattiesburg, and invited us down to go to the lagoon to watch ducks. We will probably go this weekend. We have a big lake in our front yard and especially this time of year wild ducks stop over for a few hours to a day to rest. Yesterday, right before dark, four Red-breasted Mergansers dropped in but were gone before morning. We haven't learned all our ducks yet, but are still studying and using the field guide.

Bird watching is so rewarding! I wish more people did it. This morning, before work, we were watching the Chipping Sparrows and "snow birds" eat under the feeder. Suddenly a Chipping Sparrow flew in that had a stark white head. It was solid white except for a brown spot on the top. We were really surprised! I guess it is partially albino.

We do hope you all can come to see us soon. Just give us a call, at home or at work, and drop by any time. We'd love to show you our bluebirds - if they'll cooperate. They, the bluebirds, do go rambling this time of year, but are always at home first thing and last thing every day. Hope they do have the North American Bluebird Society meeting in Jackson. That would be really exciting! Let me know what you hear. You all both take care and keep up the good work for the bluebirds.

Love,

T. and C.

February 28

Dear G. and R.

Curtis and I were really tickled to hear your news about the North American Bluebird Society coming to Jackson for their Seventh International Convention in October. We will definitely attend because bluebirds are our favorite thing in the whold wide world, and getting together with others that love bluebirds and learning about their experiences is going to be a great treat. We will spend either Friday or Saturday night at the Holiday Inn, headquarters hotel, or maybe both nights - we'll decide later so that we can attend all of the activities.

It was really flattering that you asked me to speak on the panel about our experiences feeding the bluebirds and I will be glad to do so. I have to admit that I have always avoided, whenever possible, public speaking in high school and college because I have always suffered from stage fright; but I believe I can talk myself into being brave and doing it for a subject so dear to my heart - my bluebirds. But if anyone else wants to do it instead of me, it wouldn't hurt my feelings to just sit in the audience and watch the show. However, if you need me, I will give a talk and sit on the panel.

Basically, I can tell about how we started feeding bluebirds. We picked dogwood berries and put them on an old flat stump in the yard and then when the mockingbirds and robins started eating the bluebird food and chasing away our bluebirds, Curtis built us two bluebird feeders, one for the front yard and one for the back yard, using the plans we found in *Sialia*, the magazine devoted just to our favorites. Since mockingbirds and robins could not enter the bluebird feeders, our bluebirds were safe and could enjoy their food in peace. Then we added raisins, which the bluebirds wouldn't eat at first, but after a few weeks they ate the raisins first and left the dogwood berries. This winter we fed mostly raisins and some suet and peanut hearts. I can go into a little more detail and tell about how the parents fed raisins to their babies and once the babies fledged, how they learned about the feeders and would stand on the top and hollow and flutter their wings until "Mr. Blue" went inside and got them some raisins. I could also discuss briefly the different trees, shrubs, and vines we've planted in our yard for the bluebirds' winter food needs.

We could also bring a bluebird feeder to show, and Curtis could make up some extra ones to bring to sell if you are going to have bluebird-related items for sale. Curtis just got through building a big workshop at home. He enjoys woodworking and carpentry in his spare time. He has our '76 Honda CVCC in there now reworking the motor.

We decided to do that instead of buying a new car right now, so we have been going to work in his old one for the last couple of days, waiting on some car parts to come in.

I know that you wrote the book about the Purple Martin and are interested in them, so I have to tell you that our martin scouts came Sunday, February 26, about two weeks earlier than last year. I say 'our scouts', they came to our house first but "Mr. Blue" (he has been sleeping in the martin gourds all winter and is the bluebird that claims our yard as 'his' territory) gave the martins a rude welcome. He knocked them off the porch of the martin house and chased them away. My mother lives up the hill and has a martin house, too, and the martins have been visiting both of our houses. The bluebirds always try to chase the martins off at first but soon give up. But we say, and so does mom, if we don't get martins, that is "O.K.", because the bluebirds come first for us.

We put a lot of egg shells on the egg shell board and chopped hard boiled eggs for the martins to eat yesterday during the awful snow storm and today, because it is supposed to reach a high in the low forty's. Because we were both at work all day, we aren't sure if the martins ate any of the chopped eggs, but something surely did yesterday.

Checking this weekend we found only three bluebird boxes with nest building started. They had anywhere from one-fourth to one inch of material, with our yard couple having the most. Last spring this couple started building several weeks before the other bluebirds. We are really anxious for spring, to see what rate of occupancy we get in our fifty house trail. We had put up twenty new houses this winter to add to our thirty that we already had.

Since spring is almost here, our yard bluebird couple have become more territorial and try to keep the other bluebirds out of the yard and out of the bluebird feeders. But several of them still sneak back in to get raisins out of the feeders, especially on quite cold days. On a warm day they may eat only thirty to forty raisins, but on a very cold day like yesterday, they will eat about 150-200 raisins. We don't count the peanut hearts or the suet balls that they eat.

We definitely are ready for spring! Besides the bluebird and martin houses he have two nuthatch houses in the yard. They are for the Brown-headed Nuthatches. We have lots of them and believe they will use the houses this year. They play in them and go in and out and will just sit there for fifteen minutes or more with their little heads sticking out of the entrance holes, so cute! We also put up three wood duck boxes this winter, each at a different pond on the place. We see wood ducks occasionally, but they are so shy and fly when they see us. We also put up two open-type houses for Carolina Wrens under our carport and one open-type house for an Eastern Phoebe under our front porch that is close to the lake. We have a Crested Flycatcher house ready but will wait another month before putting it up, so the bluebirds won't get too possessive of it. So you can see that Curtis has been busy this winter, building and putting up bird

8

houses. We made a few bluebird houses and sold some and gave some away this winter. So, I hope we'll get lots of tenants in our houses, but no bad kinds - no sparrows nor starlings. It is fun to see what good birds will turn up, though. This weekend we checked one of the wood duck boxes and a female flicker flew out just before Curtis climbed the ladder to look inside. It scared us both but was quite funny.

Oh, before I close, I want to tell you that we kind of borrowed your idea. Last letter you wrote you mentioned using tacks to put around the bluebird entrance holes to keep the woodpeckers from enlarging the holes. Well, Curtis bought some thin sheet metal aluminum and used a machine at his work and made plates to fit on the raccoon guards with the one and one-half inch hole made out of aluminum. That solved the problem and the plates don't bother the bluebirds. We put them on all fifty houses.

Tell Perry Ritchie that I am surely enjoying my bluebird picture that she painted for me before Christmas and have gotten many compliments on it and am looking forward to seeing her again.

One more bit of news. Evening Grosbeaks came to our seed feeders on Christmas day and haven't left yet! We must have over 100 of them, and boy can they eat! They also have bad manners! Curtis built two cages of small wire and snipped out lots of openings at the bottom just big enough for Purple Finches to go in but too small for grosbeaks. We put them on our front porch and kept a big pan filled with sunflower seeds in each so the Purple

Finches, Pine Siskins, goldfinches, etc. could eat in peace while the grosbeaks were monopolizing the regular feeders. The small birds love their 'cages' and used them right away, and have every day since - to eat in peace. I'll be glad when the grosbeaks leave! Gosh, I'm out of room! Hope you are doing well. Please come to see us in the spring or summer, and let us know what we can do to help with the convention.

Love,

T. and C.

3

Dear G. and R.

Hope you both are doing great and enjoying the spring. I wanted to tell you both what our bluebirds are up to so far. We are having a great spring - bluebird wise. We have twenty-two pairs of blue- birds on our fifty house trail, better than forty percent. We also have two chickadee nests, but one met with tragedy, then the four baby chickadees died mysteriously at nine days of age. We were very sad but pulled the nest out of the box and a bluebird couple started building in that house two days later. But the other chickadee nest is doing great so far, all six babies hatched and are growing well.

Out of the twenty-two bluebird pairs, this is how they stand as of April 30. In two boxes the babies have already fledged, eleven boxes still have babies being fed, seven have females still sitting on eggs, and two boxes have nests that are almost complete, with no eggs quite yet. The baby total is forty-six as of yesterday (two more boxes were due to hatch today) out of the thirteen boxes with hatched babies. The boxes have from two to five babies each so far. I'm glad we haven't had any with just one baby hatch. I hate for them to be so lonely! One box has white bluebird eggs, the first on the trail.

We have about twelve pairs of Purple Martins still building nests and a pair of Barn Swallows that have five babies on a wooden ledge over the carport door. They should be fledging any day because they are over two weeks old. So far we haven't lost any bluebirds, and I surely pray that we never do - to any cause. We use the STP Oil Treatment on the poles and scatter a teaspoon of sulphur dust under each completed nest to help combat the mites.

One reason I am writing you is to ask you about the Jackson Audubon Society. We subscribe to the Audubon magazine but there is not an Audubon Society close to us. We are thinking about joining the Jackson Audubon Society and the meetings to learn more and have more contact with people like us who are interested in birds. The people from the Jackson group have been so nice to us. I wanted to ask you about it because I'm sure that you belong. How do you join? How often are the meetings? What time and where are they held? Any inform-ation you can provide will be appreciated.

We belong to the Mississippi Ornithological Society and went to the spring meeting this past week in Greenville. We had a great time and saw lots of birds. I had planned to ask someone from the Jackson group about the Jackson Audubon Society, but none of the Jackson folks came. I believe someone said they had all gone to Grand Isle, Louisiana for a bird-watching week end. I'll appreciate your help.

How are the plans for the North American Bluebird Society convention going? If we can help, do let us know. I'm really looking forward to it.

I have to tell you about our "yard couple", our bluebirds that have our yard as their territory. They did get an earlier start this year. First egg was laid on March 21 and first baby bird hatched on April 7. "Mrs. Blue" laid five eggs but only three hatched. Two hatched on April 7 (Saturday), and one hatched on April 9 (Monday). Anyway, things were going great until "Mr. Blue" got sick. The babies were due to fledge on Tuesday 24 and on Friday 20 we noticed "Mr. Blue" wasn't feeding anymore. He had fed regularly before that. We noticed that he was just sitting around on the fence over in the side yard (the bluebird box is in the back yard), a good way behind the house. His wings were both drooped down and he looked quite sick. He could fly but acted as if he felt so bad and he didn't bother to fly much. He mostly just hopped up and down the fence or tree limb. But he could fly when he wanted to, so we couldn't catch him to take him to the vet.

"Mrs. Blue" fed the babies all by herself Friday through Monday. We never knew what could have gotten wrong with "Mr. Blue". He looked so sick and pitiful! I couldn't help but cry when I watched him the first couple of days. When he's well, he won't let a Blue Jay or starling in the back yard, but Saturday he watched a Blue Jay hop up and down the fence by his house and did nothing about it. Finally, "Mrs. Blue" appeared and chased off the Blue Jay.

But I wonder if "Mr. Blue" would have gotten well (I'll tell you the end of the story early - he did get well), if it hadn't been for the bluebird feeders. He was so weak and sickly, especially Friday and Saturday. He didn't even look at the ground for a bug. I don't believe he had enough energy to get a bug. He went into the bluebird feeder twice Friday to get a few raisins to eat. He was so sick looking, he even stumbled and fell down two or three times Friday and once or twice on Saturday, getting into and out of the feeder. Saturday he ate only raisins from the feeder and drank some water from the bird bath.

Sunday he was looking better. His wings didn't droop as badly and he flew more often and with longer flights, and started preening again. Monday morning he went into the feeder and ate a raisin and took one to the babies in the bird box! We were overjoyed! We jumped up and down and shouted! It was the first time he'd fed the babies or even looked at them since Thursday. By Monday afternoon he was capturing bugs and feeding both bugs and raisins to the babies. I was so grateful that he recovered! He is really our favorite of all the bluebirds. He slept in the martin gourds all winter, until the martins came. We'd watch him every evening late perching on the martin wire doing tricks catching bugs right before bed time and we'd bet on which one of the gourds he'd sleep in each night. Anyway, we were so pleased he recovered from whatever he had, and I am glad he was able to eat the raisins to keep his strength up until he licked his illness. "Mrs. Blue" worked so hard feeding the babies by herself while he was sick. She never stopped or even slowed down. She didn't even take time to bathe, preen, or rest. But a time or two each day she'd go over close to "Mr. Blue" and flutter her wings as if to show she still cared.

One baby bluebird fledged on schedule late Tuesday and the other two fledged on Wednesday. "Mrs. Blue" started on her new nest Saturday. We took out the old nest so she would build a new one. "Mr. Blue" appears to be fully recovered and is helping to tend to the babies and is courting "Mrs. Blue" heavily again since she is nest building.

The last day or so he has brought "Mrs. Blue" as much food as he has the babies. Sometimes after fluttering her wings and accepting the courtship-food gift, she'd take it to one of the three screaming babies up in the tree top. All three are doing well. We see them almost every day. One baby was down on the fence this morning. I am glad to see them finally coming down. I've looked forward to watching them learn to catch food.

I know you're probably getting eyestrain by now reading my writing, so I'll close. Take care and come see us when you can, and let us know about the Audubon meetings when you get time. Thanks.

Love,

T. and C.

Dear G. and R.

I just wanted to let you know how much we enjoyed the Mississippi Statewide Drive-in Bluebird Conference on Saturday. Our bluebirds are very dear to us and we really enjoy watching them and keeping up with our trail. I've read THE BLUEBIRD by Zeleny several times and all the issues of *Sialia* and several magazine articles on bluebirds, but I still learned a good bit at the conference and enjoyed the slide shows with the beautiful pictures. Thank you for organizing and making it possible.

Walking our bluebird trail Sunday we were particularly thrilled to see the "junior" birds from five different boxes, in the area of their boxes. These were all big enough to be out in the open on fences and lower limbs of trees learning to look for their own food but still calling and being fed by their parents.

Our couple in the yard are suppose to hatch out their second brood on Saturday. Their two juniors from the first brood keep us amused and amazed hopping around on the ground, ambushing bugs and bathing in the bird baths and still following

"Mrs. Blue" around, crying for food, even though they are able to get their own food easily.

We had a big surprise on our trail walk Sunday. We have fifty houses up in all and that doesn't cover our farm well but we plan to add more every year. One house is across the creek, over in the prairie, about one-half mile from the next house. We experimented with this house and hung it from a tree limb like one issue of *Sialia* suggested. We used thin wire, like picture wire, and hung it at least three feet below the limb so a snake, opossum, or raccoon couldn't jump from the limb to the box. By hanging it so far down from the limb it swings with the smallest breeze and really turns and swings with a good wind, but it always comes back and faces the same way when the wind quits. Every time we checked the house in early spring it had wasps in it and we saw how much it swung around so we figured that the bluebirds would never go into it, so we didn't check it every week like we did all of the other boxes. It is so far to walk and it usually takes us two and one-half hours to walk the rest of the trail, so we had not checked this house in a month.

Well, Sunday we checked it and were amazed to find a bluebird nest with four eggs in it. The female was already setting so we don't know when the eggs will hatch, since we hadn't kept a close eye on the box. It also had a wasp nest in the top of the box, and just like Dr. Jerome Jackson said at the conference, the wasps were gone and so were the larvae. The bluebirds must have chased them out and eaten the larvae.

Well, thanks again for such an interesting and informative conference. We really enjoyed it and were glad to get to see the baby bluebirds banded on the tour and hope to attend Dr. Jackson's workshop on banding. Let us know if you plan any other conferences or workshops or other kinds of meetings. We'd love to attend. Keep up the good work. I know the bluebirds would thank you if they could. If you ever get down our way, drop by and see us and our bluebirds.

Sincerely,

T. and C.

5

June 14

Dear G. and R.

Curtis and I really enjoyed your visit so much and hope you can come back soon, now that you know where we live. We did appreciate your banding our bluebirds for us. Now we can keep up with those, especially the ones in the yard, and tell them apart from the rest.

I wanted to let you know about our brood of six that you banded in our yard. Thursday (June 7) they were scheduled to fledge, so I took off work that day to watch. I sat in the yard on my bench beside the cattle gap at 7 a.m. with a big pan of green beans to snip and to watch for fledging.

The action started at 8 a.m. sharp. The first baby stuck his head way out of the box and then his body halfway out of the hole. He stayed like that for about five minutes and then flew straight down to the guard shield below the box. He sat on the shield about ten minutes and looked content to sit there all day, but the next in line stuck his head out and flew straight into the tree; so, then baby number one flew to the top of the martin house and when the martins came to investigate, he flew on down to the shield of the far martin house.

19

"Mrs. Blue" went down to keep an eye on him and "Mr. Blue" stayed by to encourage more babies out of the box. The third baby came out about 8:30 and it flew past the trees to the peak of our house, almost landed on the roof, then changed his mind and, making a U-turn, went back to the pine trees in front of the house. Meanwhile, baby number one finally flew off the martin shield into a tree. Babies four and five made it into the pine trees before ten o'clock. And one baby (I'm not sure which one because they had gotten mixed up by then) flew down to the bird bath in the back at 10:30 and drank and waded in and bathed! I couldn't believe it! I had never seen a junior blue bathe so young, but he did a good job and got out and shook off some and then flew back up into the tree. These "junior birds" have been unusual compared to the others we've watched. This new batch has spent more time down on the fence and in the bird bath. We saw them bathe several times Saturday and Sunday. Usually very young junior blues stay up high in the tree tops but these seemed to prefer the fence and the baths instead. Maybe it is the hot weather or they aren't getting enough food and have to look for their own.

Well, the story of the bluebirds has a very sad ending. How I wish I could change that! The sixth baby did not survive the weekend. To try to condense that sad tale, because it is still painful, and probably always will be to think about, I'll try to be brief. "Mr. and Mrs. Blue" tried hard all day Thursday to keep up with all the frisky babies and feed them all properly, but they didn't seem to feed the little runt left in the box much at all.

I guess they just had their hands full and were doing the best they could to keep the five that had feldged in the same area of the yard. The sixth baby was a runt. It wasn't fully developed because it was two days younger than the others, but I guess it had gotten lonely because at 6 p.m. it came out of the box. It was so small (fifteen days old) and I guess it didn't get fed as much as the others while in the box and because of its size just couldn't be as aggressive. It landed on the ground after trying to fly. We put it in the tree nearby. It tried to fly and failed again and again. So at dark we put it back in the box and Curtis put a one-inch hole reducer over the entrance hole of the box. Friday morning it hadn't gotten fed by 6:30, so we let it out of the box because we had to leave for work. It was noticed by "Mr. and Mrs. Blue" but wouldn't stay in the tree so we left it on the ground when we went to work.

I got home from work early and saw the little bird down by the bird bath in the front. I watched it for an hour and a half and it got fed one time by "Mr. Blue", so I went out and got it and brought it inside and put it in a box and we fed it according to the instructions in the Zeleny book. We caught insects all over the yard and garden for it all Friday afternoon. It was real weak at first and would just stand in one place and sleep until waked up to be fed. It might have been slightly injured because I had seen a thrasher viciously peck it for no reason at all, until "Mr. Blue" came to its rescue and I ran outside. Anyway, it looked

O.K., just tired and weak. But it seemed to perk up before dark Friday and moved around a little in the box. So, we thought it would grow stronger and we could release it in a couple of days, when it was developed enough to fly and let "Mr. and Mrs. Blue" tend to it again, But we got up Saturday morning and it was dead. We were so heart broken, so shocked, so sad! We cried and cried and buried it in the bluebird garden.

We did remove its band before burying it though. Should we mail the band back to you or do anything else with it? We were so upset because it died! It's funny how quickly you can become attached to a little bird. We loved that little bird and wanted it to live so badly! Nature seems to be so cruel sometimes. But we pulled ourselves together and decided to carry on and be thankful for all the live, healthy bluebirds that we have.

We see the five juniors several times a day now. They follow "Mr. and Mrs. Blue" around now and holler into their parents' ears for food. "Mrs. Blue" is a real glutton for punishment. She started building in the same box on Tuesday for the third brood of the year. We checked it yesterday (Wednesday) and she was almost through with the nest. I thought she might quit on two broods, since she had so many babies last time. But she has other ideas.

I got a nice note from the lady in the Jackson Audubon Society and a map of how to get to the meeting place at Belhaven College, so, if nothing goes wrong, we'll see you at the next Audubon meeting.

Our Barn Swallows over the carport entrance laid five eggs so we started checking for hatching this Sunday. We were not sure of the hatch date, though, because this is our first experience with Barn Swallows.

We checked our martins Sunday and we have sixty-three babies. So, we really have a range of ages. A few of the Purple Martin apartments had baby martins ready to fly. They were so big! Some of the nests had females still setting on eggs. But maybe they'll stay around longer this way.

We have 100 bluebird babies so far, but another box is due to hatch today and three more are scheduled to hatch Friday and one on Saturday. Monday's total should top 115 easily.

Well, I'll close now. Hope all is well and we'll see you soon.

Love,

T. and C.

July 10

Dear G. and R.

I want to tell you how much we enjoyed visiting, having dinner, and attending the Audubon Society meeting with you all. The dinner was really delicious and the drinks on your screened patio so refreshing. You have such a lovely place, with a beautiful yard full of Gray's wild flowers, with a beautiful yard and lake - right in the middle of town. It was almost impossible to believe we were in the middle of a big city. We were so tickled to get to see the Prothonotary Warblers and especially the baby warblers in the little box down by the lake. Thanks for inviting us; it was a delightful visit. Please forgive me for not writing to tell you so any sooner, but I was sort of waiting on our third bluebird brood in the yard to hatch and our baby Barn Swallows to fledge so I'd have some news to relate.

Also, now that I've stopped work (at the office, that is) and I get to stay home all the time, I can hardly pull my eyes away from the windows or prevent myself from going out in the yard to sit and bird watch, or from taking a walk on one of the trails when it is cool enough, that is, when I'm not busy cooking (I seem to be cooking more now), or shelling or putting up something out of the garden. But this is our country life and we enjoy it so much!

Our yard couple hatched out their third brood last week. One baby hatched on Monday, one hatched on Tuesday, and one hatched late Thursday. I had checked the two babies Thursday around noon and they were doing fine, so I was really shocked when Curtis checked Friday and said that another baby had hatched. The little one is so much smaller than the other two, he looks way out of place sitting beside the others. We didn't even think he would survive but we checked yesterday and all three were fine and had grown. They grow so fast. Since it is only three babies total, maybe the runt this time can compete to get his share of the food. If he does survive till fledging time, we plan to put a one inch hole reducer on the box as soon as the two big ones fledge and force the little runt to stay in the box a couple of extra days until he gets developed well enough to fly - that is, if "Mr. and Mrs. Blue" will continue to feed him. We will keep a close watch.

We had a sad episode on our bluebird trail last weekend. On Saturday we checked box number thirty-four (actually we checked all of the boxes on the trail on Saturday). It was due to hatch on Saturday and "Mrs. Blue" flew out looking fine and healthy as any bluebird. One baby had hatched that morning and another one had a small peck hole where the baby was just coming out of the shell. On Sunday afternoon I walked over to check the box number sixteen that was due to hatch. Two out of the four eggs had hatched in box sixteen. I almost never check a box two days in a row because I don't want to disturb the bluebirds too much, but for some unknown reason I decided to walk on over to box thirty-four because it wasn't far, and see if the other baby had pecked out if its shell all right.

I was horrified when I opened the box and found "Mrs. Blue" in there dead! She had her head reared back over her back in a strange position and was sitting on the nest. We think she must have had a heart attack and jerked up to fly off the nest and didn't make it. I ran home and got Curtis and we ran back to check. She was still slightly warm, so probably hadn't been dead for too long. We pulled her and the nest out and there were two babies under her; one was dead and one was still alive. So we took the baby that was still alive and put it in the box with box number sixteen's babies. We checked the next day and were so glad to see it had survived. House number sixteen had four eggs and the other two babies had hatched, so now there were five babies. This couple in box sixteen lays white eggs and this is their second brood in the same box. First brood, they had three babies, so that was an increase.

Yesterday when we checked the trail we were so glad to see all five babies in box sixteen were healthy and very big. I was preoccupied all week watching for our Barn Swallows to fledge. On Sunday morning, twenty-one days after hatching, two of them fledged. But they were so very funny! The two that fledged couldn't bear to stay away from the nest for long. They kept flying out, but after a little while would fly back into the nest. I've never seen anything like it! They'd act like they were so glad to get back in the nest. They would peck and cuddle their siblings.

We couldn't believe the two that could fly would keep coming back and getting back in the nest with the other two that hadn't flown, because they were all adult sized and the nest was so crowded with four grown up swallows. All four slept in the nest, but last night "Mr. and Mrs. Barn Swallow" slept on their extra board. This morning (the twenty-second day after hatching) all four flew. The experienced two flew about 6:00 a.m. and the younger ones at 7:30 and 7:45. The empty nest looks so sad now. I was used to seeing activity out there since mid-May and now I automatically look out there and it looks so empty.

Curtis is home now cutting grass in the front yard. As I look in the back yard I see a male cardinal, a male Indigo Bunting, and also a male quail eating under the back feeder. The red, brown, black, and white make quite a combination, and in the back there are two middle sized junior bluebirds from the second brood splashing away while "Mr. Blue" pauses in the pine with a caterpillar in his beak for the babies. I do love bird watching!

We checked our martins Sunday and only two nests (late breeders) still contain babies. All others have fledged. One set looks about five days old and the other looks about ten days old. We'll miss them when they leave.

We are going to Gulf Shores this weekend to enjoy

the ocean and salt air, and get away from the garden for a few days. But I'll miss all of our bluebirds. Our bluebird baby count to this day is 153 babies but we have six more nests due to hatch this week. Things are slowing down though and I'll be surprised if any more start on a nest this late in the summer.

We have really enjoyed all of our cardinals. Last week we had junior cardinals eating from the seed feeders from three different families. They were all different sizes and real cute. The biggest ones could crack and eat their own seeds but the smallest and middle sized are still dependent upon their parents to feed them.

All five of our middle junior bluebirds have figured out the raisin feeders and make two or three trips per day to satisfy their sweet tooth. We also put out fresh blueberries from our garden for them now in the feeders and they like those even though they are sort of big and the juniors have to take them out and bounce them on the ground a while to pulverize them to a size small enough to swallow.

Well, I better close now and get up and fry some okra for supper. Hope you all are doing great and will come back to see us soon. Curtis has some new tires ordered for the Honda to make a "dune buggy" out of it to ride the bluebird trail and he has already fixed the air conditioner in it so as soon as the tires come we can check our bluebirds in comfort and ease. Take care.

Love,

T. and C.

7

Dear G. and R.

We did miss you all at the last Audubon meeting. Glad you enjoyed your trip to Arkansas and Texas. Getting away on a vacation is always lots of fun, even though you live at a great place like you do. We really enjoyed the program at the last Audubon meeting: the slides, films, and description of rafting down the Colorado River were fantastic. We count the Grand Canyon as one of our favorite spots on earth and plan to go back. The rafting looked like great fun but I don't believe I'll ever get that much courage. We plan to attend the August Audubon meeting but not the September one because we'll be on our vacation then.

I might as well tell you about the latest tragedy in bluebird land and get it over with. It involved our yard middle juniors, the ones you banded for us. We started out with six, then the one girl died after fledging because she couldn't fly and was too weak from fledging to survive. That left one boy and four girls. We found (our favorite) the boy dead yesterday our at Curtis' big shop. He had gotten his leg band tangled in a piece of wire and we didn't see him until it was too late and I guess he starved to death. It made us both so sad! So many times I've thought 'if only I had seen him in time and could have released him!'

I didn't sleep much last night and when I did, I had terrible nightmares. I guess it is at least a one-million-to-one odds of something like that happening, so why did it happen to our junior blue? Bluebirds bring us so much joy, but also terrible heartaches. But, of course, the joys outweigh the sad times. If only I could have seen him in time! The shop isn't that far from the house and I spend a lot of time in the yard and should have heard his cries for help! It was just a small piece of wire on the weatherhead at the shop, and he had to turn his leg that particular wrong way. Fate is so cruel! I have to say that this one unfortunate accident has changed our minds about wanting to learn how to band bluebirds. I won't bother Jerry Jackson anymore about getting a permit. I'm sure that was a rare occurrence but bluebirds are so curious, exploring every little thing, and living on a farm like we do with all kinds of old sheds and equipment I'd be afraid to band any more of our bluebirds. The picture of our little blue boy dangling upside down from that wire will haunt me forever. And I guess that every time I pass the shop I'll look up at that spot and feel a sadness, a feeling of carrying a heavy burden. Anyway, I must change the subject.

Our final bluebird count for the season was a bit smaller than we had anticipated because the last few hatchings were small. I guess that's better, since late July-early August are usually very hot. Out trail produced 174 baby bluebirds. That's not counting the ten babies born in mom's house in her yard. We didn't number or count her house but we helped her check on and keep up with her babies.

We really see bluebirds everywhere we go on the farm. The juniors are so amusing now to see different ones all over the farm, because most of them are molting or changing into their adult colors and they all look different, so patchwork looking, with splotches of rust here and there and blobs of blue coming out everywhere. The rust is the most varied; some have small pale spots of rust blending in with the other larger spots and others have bold areas of rust on their chests overtaking the spots. But some young ones still have all spots. Our third brood in the yard are still all spotted. They are such a cute threesome and so brave and bold. They aren't as afraid of us as the other bluebirds are and usually let us approach within four to six feet before flying. They are also bullies and pick on the cardinals at the seed feeders, and warblers at the seed board and sometimes push around the four middle junior girls. "Mrs. Blue" fed them longer than the others. I guess because she knew it would be her last chance this year and she only stopped giving them raisins from the feeders a couple of days ago.

Even though the three are bolder and braver than the others, I don't think they're quite as bright either because they haven't figured out the feeders yet, but I'm sure it'll be any day now. They still twitter and flitter when "Mrs. Blue" goes in but she probably says, "You've been out of your box one month now. It's time to get your own food." "Mr. and Mrs. Blue" are still territorial about the yard. They'll let their offspring go into the feeders all they want to now and bathe at the bird bath all they want to, but when another bluebird comes around, a fight begins. Number four "Mr. Blue" that built right on the other side of the bluebird garden sneaks in the front feeder for a couple of raisins once or twice a day, but if "Mr. Blue" sees him, he gets attacked. They are eating about 125 raisins a day now, about the fewest during the year, but it'll pick up as the weather cools.

Glad the convention plans are coming along so well. We don't get either magazine that you mentioned. If you have either and think of it, bring them to the August meeting of Audubon for us to see. I also wanted to ask you about the correct hotel fee for one night (Saturday), for a double room so I could reserve a room - but the rates in *Sialia* were only for two nights. I also wanted to ask you about Curtis putting a couple of feeders in the display room and whether you'd be interested in our polishing up and bringing our copper bluebird fire screen to display.

We have had the rainiest summer ever and even though we still see Barn Swallows and Purple Martins in our area on occasions, we really can tell they don't spend time in the yard like they used to because of all the mosquitoes we have now. Putting on Off is a prerequisite before getting outdoors in early morning or afternoon.

We still have lots of hummingbirds and lots of birds that come and eat our suet: Pine Warblers, nuthatches, chickadees, titmice, Red-bellied Woodpeckers and downies, and the last few days we've been delighted to have a Red-headed Woodpecker. He really glows when the sun hits him and when I'm sitting out in the yard I know that he is around by his rattling voice.

Well, I better start supper now. Hope you all are doing great and we are looking forward to seeing you at the next meeting. If you need any help, let us know. Take care.

Love,

T. and C.

September 2

Dear G. and R.

I'm really enjoying watching all our bluebirds and other yard birds, since being home from the hospital. I loved them all before and watched them every chance I got but now I appreciate them even more. I miss being able to go over in the prairie or pond fields to see those bluebirds, but I can't walk that far and the ride is too rough this soon but I'll go in a couple of weeks. It is very dry and dusty here now and Curtis is having to water all the bird trees and bushes and vines, the ones that provide the winter food for the birds. Our bluebirds are eating about 100 raisins per day now out of their feeders, but they will double or triple that when winter gets here.

Our favorite time of day is between five and six in the afternoon when the bluebirds wander home to bathe, eat and fight. Anywhere from ten to thirty come every day to splash in both the front and back baths, eat bugs in the yard and garden, and perch on the power wire between the house and Curtis' shop and pounce on bugs and come to the feeders for raisins for dessert. They always fuss and fight and chase each other.

I think it is mostly play, with a purpose to prepare

34

them for spring when they will fight for real. But they get pretty tough and the bluebird chattering and fussing gets quite loud and they start chasing each other and almost run over (or into) us sitting out in the yard. I never know what to expect. It's like a three-ring circus because there are always others participating also. Usually the ground is covered with Pine Warblers hopping after bugs and turning over leaves looking for bugs and chasing each other and anything that moves. Then, too, the cardinals, titmice, nuthatches, chickadees, and woodpeckers of various kinds come into the fray. We never know what other species will turn up. But it is all so much fun to watch! We sit out quietly in the yard and feel like we're a part of it all. The birds are so used to us that sometimes they'll come within just a few feet of us to get a bug or just to perch for a while.

Well, I'll close for now. Take care and let us know if we can help in any way with the convention.

Love,

T. and C.

October 6

Dear G. and R.

Thank you so very much for the nice letter and for the program of the North American Bluebird Society Convention, to be held in Jackson. It sounds so well planned and so interesting. Even Curtis, who never comments on anything, said, "I'm going to like the heck out of that!" I've never seen him so enthusiastic about something indoors before. But a whole weekend discussing bluebirds with people who love them as much as we do, is both our ideas of a great time. I have my little speech all prepared and do have to admit I'm nervous because I never was good at public speaking. But I believe that others will be interested in hearing about our experiences feeding bluebirds. I am really glad that I get to say my part before lunch so I can enjoy and relax afterwards. We were watching a program on PBS-TV the other day and heard the announcement about the convention. You all have certainly done a great job covering the convention.

We had another terrible experience yesterday. A female bluebird hit the back window real hard and it killed her instantly. We've had it to happen to various species of birds before but this is the first time that we have had a bluebird lost like this. It was so sad and so unfair! She was so pretty, so blue. She was almost blue enough to be a male. I am going to order some of those pictures of hawks or owls out of the bird catalogue to glue on the windows.

We had a funny incident later in the afternoon with a Pine Warbler. One hit the front window (not very hard) when we were sitting out in the side yard in our favorite spot about fifty feet away. We both stood up when we saw the Pine Warbler hit the ground but it wasn't hurt too badly - it was just real groggy. But the funny thing is that when we stood up the Pine Warbler got off the ground and flew real wobbly. It lit on Curtis' shoulder! I nearly fell out with excitement and Curtis started shaking with laughter. But the warbler just stayed on his shoulder.

Now to go backwards with the story. On Wednesday a warbler hit the back window and it knocked itself out. I went out, picked it up and petted it and also put a spot of Liquid Paper (typewriter correction fluid) on top of its head. So it had a light white dot on its head. After about thirty minutes, it recovered and flew off. So, (back to yesterday) I was laughing at the warbler sitting on Curtis' shoulder and then I noticed the white spot on its head where I had put it on Wednesday. I couldn't believe it! I picked it off Curtis' shoulder and showed it to Curtis. Well, the warbler came to his senses and started hollering his lungs out. So, I let him go, because he was screaming so loudly that all of the other birds in the yard were coming to mob us. It was really funny! The warbler flew to the power line and lit unsteadily. Then it lay down on the power line wire and straddled the wire, with one leg on one side and the other on the other side of the wire, locking its toes together below. What a sight! It stayed that way for about thirty minutes and then flew to a pine tree.

Last weekend Curtis was cutting fire wood and the chain saw hit something and kicked back and cut him in the lower part of his knee. I had to take him to the emergency room at the hospital and he had to have five stitches in it. Of course that happened the last day of September. What a month! He had been in the same emergency room about two weeks ago when his eyes got burned by a welding arc. That was when I was in the hospital, and he had to go downstairs to the emergency room at midnight. But his eyes are fully recovered now and he is able to bend his knee and is even kneeling down on a cushion to do carpentry work for a friend.

Will close for now and see you both at the bluebird convention.

Love,

T. and C.

10

Dear G. and R.

Hope you all have a great Thanksgiving! I am starting my cooking tomorrow so it won't pile up on one day. We are getting excited about our delayed vacation. This time next week we are supposed to be in Cancun, Mexico. I will miss all the bluebirds but I am sure that mom will take care of them while we are gone. She always does a good job of tending to them. It is a pretty good chore to tend to three seed feeders, one suet feeder and two baths.

But the weather is getting cold here and we have been under a lot of stress lately, so I am ready to get away. We have been subjected to the constant sound of chain saws all last week and I hate the sound, and it is driving me crazy. At first it was down by the creek. At first daddy wanted to clear-cut it, but mom put her foot down and they just select - cut it. That really doesn't look too bad when they thin out the biggest trees and leave the others, so when we saw the finished product, it wasn't as bad as we'd expected, after witnessing the total destruction of clear cutting.

We really enjoyed the North American Bluebird Society International Convention in Jackson so much and you did a fantastic job making everything run so smoothly. You really could tell it was so well planned. My only regret is that I didn't examine the bluebird gift shop earlier! By the time I went shopping in there I missed some real good bluebird buys. But I am proud of my small carving of the bluebird by Matthew Renna that I bought. It looks real cute on our shelf with the miniature wooden nest box next to it, the one that we were given by the Jackson group as table favors at the banquet that night. Somebody certainly did a lot of work making about 300 of those little houses, so nicely painted white with blue tops.

Our bluebirds are really eating more now that the weather has gotten cooler. They had cut down to about twenty-five raisins per day a few weeks ago when it was real warm and wet, but now they are eating eighty to ninety raisins per day and will increase even more in the next few weeks I'm sure. They still haven't eaten any of the bluebird food that we got at the convention (the trial pellets), even though we kept three or four in each feeder. I don't think that they are going to eat the pellets as long as they have the raisins there, and we will never deprive them of their raisins, since they love them so much. So, I guess we can't be counted in the experimental run of this new food. I even occasionally see (when I'm inside the house and watching closely with binoculars) a bluebird eating eight to ten peanut hearts instead of, or in addition to, the raisins.

One of our bluebirds has the funniest sleeping spots, we discovered. Last summer when some baby king-birds fell out of the nest, we tried to rig up a makeshift nest for them. We took a little old black plastic flower pot (the kind with holes around the bottom) and cut it off about seven inches high and hung it in the small pine tree right across from the yard cattle-gap. Well, one male bluebird (so far) sleeps in the old flower pot at night. Last night I watched him go to bed in it. He was so funny! He kept looking out and then dropping down again into the bottom. The wind was blowing real hard and his 'bed' was rocking back and forth but he finally quit peeking out and settled down to sleep. I guess he got rocked to sleep.

Glad both of you all are doing better with your ailments. It really seems to take forever to get well sometimes I know. I didn't have any problems from my surgery but my arthritis and bursitis bother me terribly at times and I get out the aspirins and the heating pad for a couple of days and then it lets up some and then the cycle starts all over again. But I just try to be thankful every day for what isn't hurting and try not to concentrate on what is hurting.

Take care and try to come see us sometimes over the Christmas holidays. Just give us a call; we'd love to have you come and we could ride around in the "dune buggy" and look for bluebirds.

Sincerely,

T. and C.

11

Dear G. and R.

Just received your lovely card today. I surely hope this letter reaches you before Christmas. Please forgive me for sending it this late. Going on vacation in November put me behind on all my holiday shopping, cooking, mailing out cards, etc. I spent the morning cooking and am finally catching up.

Sure hope the doctor gives you the O.K. to toss those crutches aside. I know that it would make your Christmas, but be careful and not overdo. My arthritis has been bothering me all week so I've turned to the aspirins and heating pads again.

Our trip was a lot of fun! The Carribbean is just beautiful, with crystal clear water in shades of aqua. We snorkled, swam, walked on the beaches, went deep sea fishing (Curtis caught barracuda and Spanish Mackerel - I just watched), swimming, shopping and went on a tour to see Chichen-Itza ruins and did some bird watching. We saw lots of multi-colored, exotic tropical birds, but none could compare with our bluebirds. We saw lots of varities of hummingbirds in all shapes and colors. But we did have lots of stomach problems, even though we took medicine along (especially me), so we plan to vacation in the U.S.A. for a while.

Our bluebirds are eating about ninety raisins per day but that will increase when it gets cooler again. We are enjoying the warm weather and so are the bluebirds because the bugs are out. The availability of bugs has so much to do with the number of raisins the bluebirds eat.

We are tentatively planning an overnight trip New Year's Day to either Jackson, Memphis, or New Orleans to celebrate our eighth wedding anniversary on New Year's Day. We thought we'd get away for the night, stay in a hotel with a heated pool indoors, and eat out and celebrate our anniversary. We are talking about coming to the Christmas bird count with the Jackson Audubon folks (we've never been to one), but haven't decided yet. Curtis is supposed to find out this week if he gets an extra little job wiring a friend's house. So, if he gets that job, I don't guess we'll get to the coast. He likes doing any type of carpentry or electrical work.

Now that winter is here we have lots of starlings around and this week we've even seen several House Sparrows on the place. I've tried to shoo them away but haven't had much luck yet. I do dislike starlings and sparrows!

I surely hope you all come by to see us over the holidays. We'd love to see you! Just give us a call so we'd be sure to be here. Hope you both are feeling fine and that you have a great Christmas.

Love,

T. and C.

12

Dear G. and R.

Hope that you both are feeling good and surviving this rough winter weather. All our bluebirds seem confused lately. One day it gets up to fifty degrees, then they'll be playing on their houses and going in and out of them and singing and fluttering their wings fiercely, and the next day the high will be twenty degrees and they don't waste energy moving about much. They just fluff out their feathers fully and search intently for the occasional insect.

Our yard bluebirds are fat and spoiled from eating in their feeders. They eat 150-250 raisins a day, depending on the weather. When the weather allows, I go walking around the farm and check on different boxes and clean them out. Bluebirds are sleeping in quite a few of them now and the houses get spoiled quickly. About three weeks ago we moved about ten houses that had been unproductive because the weeds got so high around them in the summer, or for some other reason. We didn't put out any new ones, but tried to move them to better spots. We have two bluebirds (at least) that are sleeping in the martin gourds in the back yard (our yard "Mr. and Mrs.") and one or two sleep in a flower pot in a pine tree.

We are having trouble with House Sparrows trying to move in and they are so hard to drive away. I did get lucky and hit one male that was eating in the backyard feeder. It also cracked the plexiglass but Curtis patched it with clear library tape and was glad that I hit the sparrow. Last week we saw a pair out at Curtis' shop and we figured out that they were sleeping in the tin plate that has a curve at the top. Curtis went out there at eight o'clock one night. It was pitch dark and about zero degrees, with the chill factor included, and he planned to stuff a piece of cloth in the hole and trap them, and those awful things flew out in the pitch dark, freezing weather and got away, right before he could stuff in the cloth.

We have lots of birds at our feeders but I don't guess the Purple Finches are coming this year. We've also missed the Pine Siskins at the feeders, but are glad the Evening Grosbeaks didn't come this year. They like to have eaten us out of house and home last year, so we didn't mind their absence. We put up the thistle feeder last week and the goldfinches came in droves. Thistle seed is so expensive that we might take the feeder down if they keep on eating so much thistle feed. Really, could I do that!

This weather is certainly comething! It was so warm and dry during December. We planted our English peas early, also some spinach and onions. All came up but just froze when the January freezes started. I'm sure the spinach and onions

45

died right away and don't have much hope for the English peas either.

Well, I just wanted to drop you all a line to let you know we are thinking about you. We are still waiting on you all to drop by and see us whenever you can. We'd love to see you. I can't wait till spring! This cold weather isn't for birds or people. I seem to develop new problems each week. Now I'm having trouble with my back. But maybe it will look up when it warms up. I can't wait till nest building time and am looking forward to seeing the martins. Take care and stay warm and dry.

Love

T. and C.

13

Dear G. and R.

Missed you all at the February Audubon meeting. The program was interesting, slides and
information about Africa. It reminded us of some
of the PBS nature shows. Hope you are both
feeling well and didn't miss the meeting because of
illness.

Things are really beginning to happen here,
bird things. Our yard bluebird couple have been
courting and mating for a couple of weeks, real
heavily, and "Mrs. Blue" started building yesterday, about a week ahead of her last year's schedule. But like she always does for her first brood,
she is building slowly to start with and building in
more than one box. I saw all of her activity
yesterday morning and checked after lunch and
the bottoms of two boxes were covered with dried
grass and fibers pulled off the cedar fence rails.
She is building in number two, the house in the
backyard that was home to all three of their
broods last year, and number three, the house
painted white at the end of the vegetable garden
behind Curtis' shop. I haven't noticed any other of
the bluebirds building yet, but our "Mrs. Blue" in

the yard is always first. The raisins must be responsible for our "Mr. and Mrs. Blue's" extra energy.

Also, our martin scouts came today. They were exactly one week later this year than last year. I looked out there a few minutes ago and there were three black males and one female(?) here so far, and "Mr. Blue" was furious and was chasing them off right and left. The same thing happened last year and I was scared that the martins would leave for good, but they persisted and "Mr. Blue" finally accepted them. But he never accepts and always chases House Sparrows. If only all blue-birds were as aggressive as he is! We have had several House Sparrows this year and have a hard time getting rid of them, but we keep trying and have killed about six since the first of the year - but there is still one pair to get rid of. Darn sparrows!

I saw a male cardinal yesterday hull a sunflower seed at the back feeder and fly to the back fence to feed it to a waiting female. So, they are courting already, too. I just hope that the weather doesn't get extremely cold again and hurt all the early nesters and the martins' bug supply. Have your martins arrived yet?

We are planning on going this week with the Jackson group to the Atchafalaya Basin in Louisiana. We have never been camping or canoeing before, so it will be a real experience. I am having just minor aches and pains with my hips and back but really doing pretty well, so I hope I can hold up. We aren't getting any younger, so we decided to give it a try and have heard it is so pretty down there and we are ready to get away for a couple of days.

We have had about ten inches of rain in the last couple of weeks. I guess you all are the same way. Hope your lake hasn't risen too much. We still have all the winter birds, species wise, but the number of individuals has decreased. We had about 200 goldfinches at the feeders at the peak of the winter season, but now they have decreased in number, though we still have some of them, along with a good many Pine Siskins.

We missed the Purple Finches this year. Did you all have many winter birds at your feeders this year? We had (for the first time this year) a couple of Fox Sparrows and Field Sparrows at our feeders as well as Rufous-sided Towhees.

Hope all is going well for both of you and that your bluebirds are doing great. Take care and visit us or write when you get a chance.

Love,

T. and C.

14

Dear G. and R.

It was real good to hear from you both and also a coincidence, because when we went to the Mississippi Ornithological Society meeting in Vicksburg this past weekend and stopped in Jackson late Friday afternoon for a bit of shopping, I called your house to see if you all were getting well and just to talk a few minutes before heading for Vicksburg. But I didn't get an answer. I have been thinking of you both and meaning to write for a long time, but I haven't stopped long enough to do both. All my correspondence is behind and my magazines are going unread by the half-dozens. We did miss the last Audubon meeting because the weather was bad and Curtis had to go to the dentist and hated to get off work early again.

We have been doing a bit of birding with the Jackson "field trip regulars". We went to Dauphin Island last month, on the Alabama coast, and are going to try to go this coming weekend to see Red-cockaded Woodpeckers above Louisville, MS with the Jackson folks. Dr. Jerry Jackson of Mississippi State University is leading the group. The poor garden needs so much attention, but we are so busy checking and tending to our bluebirds.

Our bluebirds are doing great. We counted (as of last Thursday) ninety-one babies for the first broods, and all haven't hatched yet. We have thirty bluebird couples in forty-eight houses. We took a couple of houses down. We have one pair of titmice and one nest that looks like a wren nest. We haven't checked this week, might have thirty-one or thirty-two couples.

Our yard couple got started about a week earlier this year on their first brood. The babies fledged April 19 and 20 (five babies). We had a very unusual occurrence that took place which was most interesting. I'll try to detail it. Our yard couple (the same ones we've had for the past three years) stay in the yard and eat lots of raisins and have lots of babies. We have spent so much time watching them over the past three and one-half years that we know them on sight by their mannerisms - like, how they bathe, where they like to perch, and even how they go into the raisin feeders. They built their nest for the first brood and acted as normal as usual except for one thing, one of their children from last year, I know because you had banded her, one of the middle girls from the middle brood, didn't leave the yard.

All the while "Mrs. Blue" was building, sitting on eggs, etc. for the first brood middle girl (MG for short) hung around and "Mrs. Blue" didn't chase her off like "Mr." and "Mrs." did all the other bluebirds. The three of them would often sit together or at least within close view of one another. Anyway, when "Mrs. Blue's" babies hatched out in the back yard, MG started building a nest in the front yard all by herself. We thought she was crazy and "Mrs. Blue" just ignored her. But "Mr. Blue" (her father) started paying closer attention.

Well, MG laid five eggs and we were shocked because we knew that there were no other male bluebirds permitted in the yard. About ten days after "Mrs. Blue's" babies fledged, MG's babies hatched. In the meantime we saw "Mr. Blue" hanging out with both the girls and I even saw "Mr. Blue" leave "Mrs. Blue's" side in the yard and fly over and mate with MG in front of "Mrs. Blue" and two of her newly fledged babies looking on. "Mrs. Blue" finally got mad this time and she jumped on "Mr. Blue" when he flew from MG and they fought briefly, with MG watching. But now the amazing part. MG's babies hatched on Monday and "Mr. Blue" was still very busy feeding his newly fledged family of five and "Mrs. Blue" was starting her nest for her second brood and wanted to court and "Mr. Blue" had three newly born ones to feed. He fed them very little but some, and fed MG and "Mrs. Blue" and his first five babies. Tuesday morning the incredible thing happened - a new male bluebird came up and adopted MG and her family!

I was outside that Tuesday and watched the whole thing. All four adult bluebirds had a staring contest on the side fence and the new "Mr." fluttered and swooned over MG and "Mr. Blue" and "Mrs. Blue" looked relieved and let them live in peace in the front yard. The new male fluttered with MG about an hour and she was very submissive and let him mate with her as she searched for food for the babies. By noon he was allowed to look in MG's box at the babies and he was surprised and confused. He went in the box several times Tuesday afternoon and often took in pine straw or fence fibers as if he was building a nest. MG always let him do just as he pleased with her and the babies. I saw him taking building materials in the box (only small pieces) all that day and often he would come out with a new piece. He brought out a feather that MG had lined the nest with one time.

I decided to leave them alone. By Wednesday morning he was bringing food to her box but was still confused and would often eat it before going in the entrance hole. But by Wednesday afternoon he was going straight in with food. He was a strange bluebird and followed MG constantly the first few days whenever she came out of the box - courting her. It took him three days to get up the courage to try the front bath after watching his new wife bathe often and he watched her go in the front bluebird feeder. Finally he tried that after five days and several false starts. Anyway, all is fine now and the two pairs of bluebirds get along very well and don't fight. It is really entertaining!

"Mrs. Blue" is building in number two for her second brood and I saw her some but was watching the front couple (MG and her new hubby) more. I shouldn't even tell you this, but I will. We had meant to take down house number three, in our vegetable garden, because it was too close to number two (our "Mr." and "Mrs." home in the back) and because Curtis uses the tractor and makes lots of noise at his shop sometimes, but we just hadn't gotten around to taking it down. Anyway, I looked in number three house and was shocked to see "Mrs. Blue" had built a nest out there, too, and had laid her first egg in it Thursday morning. I was in a quandary but made a decision and carried it out. I moved nest and egg, all into number two and Thursday afternoon Curtis took number three down. I was feeling guilty but we left Friday for Vicksburg anyway. I was so relieved Sunday when I came home and saw "Mrs. Blue" had accepted my moving her nest and had tightened up the nest and laid more eggs in it.

We have lots of martins this year and not as many hummingbirds. We put up boxes for the Prothonotary Warblers but didn't get any. You are the lucky one with the "prothos". We had bad luck with our nuthatches. Their eggs were infertile. Last year they hatched in fourteen days and this year "Mrs. Nut" was still setting after twenty-eight days, so we removed the eggs and hope that she will lay some more. We had Carolina Wrens build in a house that Curtis put up for them on the porch and they fledged five young ones. Our carport Barn Swallows came back and added about one inch of mud to their old nest and lined it with feathers that I put under the carport roof for them to use. We are expecting the first egg any day now.

I was so upset this morning when I went by mom's. She hadn't seen her bluebird couple (the babies would have been twelve days old today) much over the weekend and wanted me to check her house with her. We opened it and inside was a huge rat snake. It had eaten all five of the babies! Even though the house was on PVC pipe. How awful!

We must have the seventeen year (or whatever it is) outbreak of locusts. There seem to be millions of them over in the woods and across the prairie, just covering everything. But so far we can't see any damage. When we step out of the house, the sound is so eerie, like the "Twilight Zone", and when we go down into the woods, the sound is deafening. I hope they don't interfere with the bluebirds. We have even seen bluebirds eating these huge locusts and found parts of undigested locusts in the bluebird boxes. It is incredible that the bluebirds are feeding these huge insects to their babies.

We have had a large flock of Bobolinks around the house the last week and have enjoyed watching and listening to them.

I had better close for now.

Love,

T. and C.

15

Dear G. and R.

Isn't this weather awful? We haven't had any rain since May and this terrible heat wave that won't let go is so severe. I've been staying inside in the air conditioning but really feel sorry for the poor birds. We have been watering our yard and garden daily. Our bluebirds in the back, number two house with the second brood, were supposed to fledge Thursday but all four fledged Tuesday, two days early. We figured it was because it was so hot. None could fly very well and landed on the ground and we had to put them all back up in the tree several times. Even Wednesday morning I had to put one back into the tree. But Wednesday evening we did see all four in the tree doing very well.

Usually they'll fly up very high a couple of hours after fledging, but these all stayed low in the tree for over a day. I guess they weren't really developed enough to fly far; but I believe they'll be all right. We didn't have the heart to put them back in that hot house!

I was sorry to hear about the snake getting all of your Purple Martins! We've had a real bad year - snake wise, too. I believe the day after I wrote last,

56

telling you about middle girl in the front and her new husband feeding and adopting her babies, we had disaster, too. We checked the box the next day after seeing MG and her husband acting strange, and it was empty. A snake must have gotten in late that afternoon and by morning, no babies. We were sick when we discovered it that afternoon! The box (it was the first time it had been used by bluebirds in three years) must have had too small a shield to protect it. We took it off the fence immediately and put up one on a piece of PVC on the other side of the fence. Middle girl was very accepting and started rebuilding her nest within thirty minutes in the new box. So, it was a sad happening but she was very determined to have babies again soon and now she does. Her babies (four of them) are ten days old now and getting fed to pieces by their proud parents. Before the babies fledged in the back we had a week long period where we had baby bluebirds in the front and back at the same time for the first time ever.

We have 160 baby bluebirds on our trail so far, but four boxes were scheduled to hatch today. I haven't checked them yet because it is so hot to walk and I'll get Curtis to drive me around when he comes home from work. We should get 200 this year, if the weather breaks. I hope it won't affect hatching or the babies health.

We are enjoying the Barn Swallows again this year. Their brood of four is about twelve days old and keep the carport lively. I can watch them being fed and tended to from the window in the dining room or through the window in the kitchen door and it is almost like being in the nest with them.

We checked our martins again this week and have eighteen pairs. Some babies were ready to fledge and some pairs were still setting on the eggs. There were over sixty baby martins in the gourds so far. Ours seem to be "O.K." so far, but this morning I was walking by mom's and saw her martins going crazy about something, so I went over there thinking it was a snake. The heat must have driven them out early. We got the ladder and put three of them back in the box in the house but the fourth was too far gone. I tried to save it but it had fire ants on its body in such numbers that it died in about ten minutes. I got off all the fire ants I could, but it had been so bitten that it was impossible for it to stay alive. Our martins have been eating record numbers of egg shells this year. It is so dry that we do not have many mosquitoes.

We missed you all at the last meeting. It was the first pot-luck dinner one that we had attended. The food was really great and the speaker was inspiring also.

I can understand your battle with squirrels. They are very smart creatures! Our Fox Squirrels still come around some and the martins and Barn Swallows hate them and attack them furiously. The Barn Swallows are the worst. When the squirrels come under the carport, the swallows holler so loudly that I can hear them with all the windows shut, the air conditioners on, the dish washer going, and the television going full blast. Then I know it is time for me to help out. So, I ran out and chase off the squirrel.

I hope you did get some martins, but if you didn't, you'll surely get some next year. I really despise snakes!

Hope you all are doing better and do come to see us when you're up to it. Don't worry about bringing anything, I'll fix a "garden lunch"; that's what we live on in the summer time. Gardens are so much trouble that we try to do them justice by eating as much as we can from the garden. So, just give us a call and come when you can. Hopefully, it will cool off one day. July just has to be better than June! Last summer we didn't cut on our air conditioning until July and this summer is was May.

Take care and stay cool indoors.

Love,

T. and C.

16

Dear G. and R.

We were so glad to hear about the Barn Swallows nesting on top of the entrance lights of your motel in Estes Park, Colorado. They are about our most favorite bird, behind the bluebirds. We enjoyed our's nesting under the carport this summer but were heart broken when the babies from the second brood and adults suffered a disaster. At least the first brood's four babies survived. The second brood (this is the first year the adults attempted two broods) was eleven days old. The four babies were doing great, being fed by their parents very often.

It was a Tuesday and I left about 1 p.m. to do some shopping. I met Curtis when he got off work and we went to the movies. We got home about 7 p.m., to find it was raining there. As soon as we drove under the carport we noticed immediately that we didn't see the baby heads hanging over the nest. We grabbed a stool and checked and there was only one baby left in the nest, and it was dead. We found two more dead babies in the gravel beside the carport entrance, already covered with fire ants. We figured the other one was dead somewhere. The only explanation to what could have happened is that our neighbors must have used some poison spray somewhere close and the adult Barn Swallows must have picked up some bugs and ate them and died.

The babies must have crawled out of the nest in hunger. It was so terrible and sad! We had enjoyed these birds immensely! The only bright light in the story happened about 7:30 p.m. It was dark because it was raining. I went back outside and just happened to see, behind an old shoe box, a baby Barn Swallow. Curtis couldn't believe I had found it because it was so dark. This baby Barn Swallow was the only one that had fallen out of the nest and crawled toward the kitchen door instead of the gravel. He had fallen on that hard concrete and crawled all the way and had been without food for hours. He was very weak and we fed him some puppy food (good quality food that we had on hand for bird emergencies) and some hard boiled egg yolk. I called Dr. Jerry Jackson at Mississippi State University and asked him what to do and he recommended putting him in a nest with other baby Barn Swallows, if we could find one under a bridge.

We were surprised but glad the next morning to find that baby swallow was still alive. We fed him some more and loaded up the truck with ladders and took off to search for Barn Swallow nests. After climbing up on the shaky ladder and checking about a dozen nests, with no luck, Curtis finally found a nest that had two babies in it that appeared to be about two days older than ours, as close as we could tell.

Curtis but baby Barn Swallow up in the nest and climbed down the ladder. He (baby swallow) immediately climbed to the edge of the nest as if he was fixing to jump. I suggested to Curtis that he climb back up and put the baby under the other two. He did, and the baby swallow settled down right away and even closed his eyes for a nap. We went back that afternoon and again the next afternoon and baby Barn Swallow was doing fine. We could tell him from the other two because ours still had peach fuzz on his head and the other two had slick heads.

We miss having them under the carport so much and hate that so many of them died. The mosquitoes appeared under the carport the very next day - the "barns" had kept them eaten up.

Our bluebirds had a prosperous year. We have had 273 babies hatched out this year and there still is one box to check for hatchings. They had their share of problems but I believe the majority have made it. We had three broods in both the front and back yards this year - a real treat to have so many so close to the house for us to see regularly. They are all still eating raisins when the yellow jackets aren't in the feeder. We declare war on the yellow jackets and swat them all day long.

Well, I had better close. Take care and let us know when we can get together. Hope all goes well and to see both of you soon.

Love,

T. and C.

17

Dear G. and R.

We have gotten on the ball - picture wise, especially Curtis. You would be proud of him! He built a blind out of plywood from which to take pictures. I tried to stay in it several times and never lasted too long, forty-five minutes, tops - on a cool day. The blind is smaller than a phone booth and if it is ninety-five degrees outside, it is at least one hundred and five degrees inside, with no breeze blowing at all. So, sitting there motionless in that oven takes a hearty fellow. Curtis is good at sitting still and he is tolerant. I kidded him that I hardly saw him this weekend, that he spent all the weekend in the blind taking pictures, in pursuit of the perfect picture. But he has made a remarkable discovery and should have some great pictures.

Do you remeber the last bluebird house down by the lake? Well, the babies were born (three of them) on August 1. We knew that they were the only babies left in the box, so Curtis took the blind down there Sunday to try and get some good close-ups of them feeding. And he discovered that the three babies were being fed by three juniors and no adult bluebirds were seen.

63

Curtis must have spent close to three hours down there yesterday and saw (and took pictures of) two junior males and one junior female feeding. The junior feeders must be from the first brood because they still had spots in the throat area but their chests were turning rusty. We don't know what happened to the adult birds. Curtis said that the behavior of the junior feeders was fascinating. We have spent years watching our yard bluebirds and know the courting behavior so well after witnessing it hours upon hours. The fluttering of wings, the soft warbling to each other, etc. Curtis said that the two males, the junior feeder males, would sit on the top of the power wire and warble and flutter gently to each other and would often bring food at the same time and sit on top of the box, each with food, and gently talk and 'flirt' with each other taking turns feeding the babies. I was utterly amazed and cannot wait to see pictures that he took. We had gotten a couple of rolls of black and white film for the camera to take some shots from inside the blind. We took a roll of b/w and then changed to color and took some color shots. I just can't wait to see them! I pray that the camera, film, and/or developing doesn't mess up on these.

We had read numerous times of young bluebirds feeding box babies but never have seen it occur in our yard boxes and we have never been at the right place at the right time to witness this on our trail before. Seeing is believing! I think that bluebirds are very remarkable birds to help out each other like this.

Like 'icing on the cake', a real coincidence! I witnessed another episode (with a slight variation) of older juniors feeding young ones. While walking early this morning to the prairie, (I usually go for my 'two miler' down the road, since I can avoid the deep grass, and I wear my tennis shoes for comfort) but this morning I felt like going to the prairie so I pulled on my galoshes, sprayed Off on my pants legs to discourage the prairie ticks, and grabbed my sun visor and binoculars.

As always, there were bluebirds everywhere, especially juniors, to look at and slow down my walking speed. I was amused when a humming-bird almost ran over me midway of the old chicken house behind mom's and dad's house. It was in such a hurry that I stopped to watch it with my binoculars as it sped across the field, over the little pond, towards our house and the two quarts of hummer feed on the front porch. They must come from miles to our house, even though it is mid August. They are still eating close to two quarts of food a day. There are so many of them. Anyway, to get back to the original subject, as I was walking closer to the trees around box number thirty-five, I heard the unmistakable sound of little juniors begging for food. I stopped immediately, because it is always a thrill to see little juniors being fed, even though I have seen it a million times before.

But I was so amazed to see those little juniors still with huge white rings (bug eyes they only have when real young) and short, stubby tails, less than an inch long, flittering and being fed by two older juniors. The older juniors still had most of their spots but were beginning to get blotches of rust on their chests. I watched the two older juniors feed the babies two times and then when one of the older juniors flew on the ground for the third time and decided to take his insect off to eat it himself, I suppose, the three little juniors took off in hot pursuit to try and get the food and I lost sight of the whole bunch up in the tree tops chasing around. So, I continued on my walk, glad to have seen such a sight. When I got to my turn-around point on the prairie, I was pleased to see a flock of fourteen wild turkeys - so it was a good outing. We never let anyone shoot the turkeys.

I suppose that the older siblings feeding the younger siblings goes on more often than I had imagined in the bluebird world. It just amazes me and is another example that bluebirds are not just pretty to look at but are also very smart, compassionate, and fascinating.

We have taken a good many pictures (mostly Curtis has), some color and some b/w, but haven't gotten any back yet. We hope to see some good ones. If you come to the August Audubon meeting, we will try to bring any pictures that we have developed to show you. If we come, we will try to get there early enough to give you all a call between six and six-thirty to see if you are at home and are coming to the meeting. If you are not coming, we will either bring the pictures by or get you to meet us somewhere, like Highland Village to give them to you.

Our final bluebird count for the season comes to 276 babies, more than we had imagined. In 1983 there were seventy-seven, in 1984 there were 174, and now 276. With good care and proper attention bluebirds really increase rapidly. I was pleasantly surprised last Thursday morning when I was outside early and heard martins. I hadn't seen any for a couple of weeks, so I was glad to see six sitting on our TV antenna (their favorie perch) talking. I think they were telling me good-bye.

Our yard birds finished off the Concord Grapes in the yard and now they have started on the muscadines near the Concords. They are mostly cardinals, tanagers, and thrashers, but we were surprised yesterday to see our Fox Squirrels eating the muscadines, and they would not even run away when we beat on the window only a few feet from them. First the blueberries, and now the muscadines! Those squirrels will eat anything! The bluebirds are enjoying the bumper crop of pokeberries this year. Saturday morning we walked over to the cutover where there are thickets of briers, pokeberries and so on, and we must have seen over 100 bluebirds eating pokeberries, flying down in the bordering field for bugs, flying off, calling and chasing each other. They seemed to be having such fun.

Curtis had taken the camera but didn't get any pictures because they wouldn't let us get close enough for any really good shots. I wish the little critters would be tamer sometimes! Or at least we could declare a truce. I wish I could tell them and they could tell me, "You all let us get real close and take good pictures of you and hey, even sit on our shoulders, and we promise not to tell or expect it of you again, and we will reward you with more raisins and more houses and Curtis will keep your grass cut extra short for good bug hunting." If only...Well, that's the stuff of which fantasies are made.

Love,

T. and C.

18

August 22

Dear G. and R.

Your letter about the hummingbirds that were trapped in the ceiling area of the automobile repair department of your local chain auto place reminded me of an experience that we had with hummers.

It is about a female hummer that we tried to catch. In the early summer we had a female that came regularly to one of the feeders but this time she had a mass of cobwebs and small debris tangled around one foot. It hung down in a fat stem from her foot, at least as long as she was. We watched her for over a week, hoping she would dislodge the load and marveled at how she could fly with all that weight. Finally we tried to intervene. Curtis thought that he could catch her with his bare hands and he spent a couple of hours standing motionless at the feeder. He is quick, but not that quick! I tried to tell him it was a waste of time. Then I got some cheesecloth and a coat hanger and dental floss and tried to make a net to catch her with. We both imitated statues and tried that approach several times but she always slipped away. It was fun to stand with her only inches away from our face at the feeder. You ought to try it sometime.

After a couple of minutes the hummers accept your presence and come to eat. Even hummers look big that close up and watching them is fascinating. Some would be very curious (always females) or maybe brave, and buzz about two inches from our eyeballs, hovering closer until our reflexes would take over and we would shut our eyes and laugh. I don't know whether their purpose was to scare us off, make us "crack up", or see if the iris or pupil of our eyes was edible. But, anyway, we never could catch the 'over weight' female hummer with the entanglement and eventually gave up. We were relieved, when, after about three weeks, she came to the feeder one morning with the debris shortened by half, and after about another week we could barely recognize her because it was only about the length of a pea. We don't know how she got herself stuck up to start with or how she finally got it removed after carrying it around for over a month. We really felt sorry for her and wanted so much to help when we saw her struggling so; especially after a rain when she and her cobweb mass were wet, she could hardly lift off, and we wondered how she could migrate back across the Gulf to her winter home. So, we were very glad when she healed herself.

I believe a few of our hummers (maybe one-fourth of them) have left for points south, but I still see a few males. The males usually leave first. There is a female that guards the back yard salvia, usually perching on the clothes line. She is very aggressive and sits on her perch, constantly turning her head from side to side, looking for in-truders. When another hummer enters her terri-tory, or even a butterfly, she zooms in for the attack and banishes the intruder. But sometimes she doesn't stop with picking on someone her own size and we have laughed at her many times when we have seen her chasing off cardinals and Pine Warblers that got too close to her salvia bush. It is really funny to see a big bird like a cardinal fleeing from the back yard with a tiny hummer in hot pursuit. But I've never seen her go after a bluebird. I guess she knows her limit, because bluebirds, especially juniors, are tough and will fight back.

We always laugh at the juniors; year after year, brood after brood, they follow the same behavior patterns. When they are at least two weeks old out of their boxes (at least two weeks after fledging) until they get taught a good lesson, they like to test their independence and strength by picking on some of the other bird species in the yard. It is just part of their growing up process.

Late yesterday afternoon, after I got out of the shower, I looked out in the front yard to see if anything was in the pyracantha bush that is covered with orange berries and a popular place for several species. I picked up my binoculars off the bed (I take them from room to room in the house all day until dark because I never know when I'll want to get a close-up view of something out one of the windows) when I saw a tanager eating berries. He was quite pretty, yellow all over except for his head that was a shade of yellow, orange, and red. As I was watching the tanager, a junior blue flew in from the side yard and chased the tanager out of the bush. The tanager went to the fence for a minute and then flew back to the bush on the opposite side of the junior blue. It made no difference to the junior. She again chased the tanager off. This time the tanager left the yard.

Junior blue came back to the bush and tasted and spit out two pyracantha berries before he found two that pleased him enough to swallow them. Then junior looked over at the feeder where the cardinals were eating. She flew to the feeder and knocked the one cardinal off that was on that side, then happily hopped around to the other side to do the same to the three remaining cardinals. But her big eyes opened wider when one of the cardinals met her at the corner and called her bluff, causing junior to fly off to the fence to nurse her hurt feelings. I doubt if that was enough to teach that particular girl a lesson. Usually it takes several encounters before they learn to quit being bullies and mind their own business.

Sitting out in the yard, with morning coffee or afternoon soda, Curtis and I have seen junior blues get a real education from kingbirds. Eastern Kingbirds can be very fierce, especially when pushed, and many times we have seen junior blues jump on kingbirds for no reason. It takes but one lesson from a kingbird to teach a junior blue some manners, because kingbirds always fight back. One time the two birds fell to the ground fighting constantly and the kingbird was the first to get up. Usually the junior blue will lie on the ground for a few seconds longer, probably wondering what hit him. But I'll bet that particular junior blue never picks on a kingbird again, and hopefully doesn't pick on any other bird that doesn't deserve it.

Another behavior pattern we enjoy in each brood of yard juniors is their cuddling and the part that is particularly amazing is that the different broods each season choose the same favorite 'play spots', or as we call them 'cuddling spots' because that is what the junior blues do there. One favorite spot is the old telephone pole in the side yard where the martin house used to sit years ago. On top of this big pole is a pair of two by four pieces of wood that form a cross. The junior blues love to get in the corners where the two pieces meet on top of the pole. Anywhere from two to five juniors will cuddle with each other, pushing each other tighter against the corner, hopping on top of each other and stealing the middle spot, picking and preening on each other.

Another favorite spot they frequent is up under the aluminum martin house on top of the bracket that holds the wooden martin house. This is a space of about six inches high that the juniors really enjoy. The martin house overhead blocks off the sun so I can often see them cuddling there even in the heat of the day in their shaded play spot. The third favorite spot chosen by each brood every year is on the power wire that goes out to Curtis' shop. At the power pole there is a wooden bracket that the wire rests on and the wooden bracket is a special toy of the juniors. Curtis and I have shared many laughs watching the junior antics out on the shop wire bracket. Young bluebirds spend more time playing and having fun than any other birds that I've seen and they are so funny to watch.

The birds did us a favor this morning. After breakfast we looked out the back to see what the bluebirds were up to and we saw about four bluebirds and about six cardinals in the blueberry bushes, all acting strangely. The bluebirds were hovering like hummingbirds and the blueberry bushes were full of cardinals, all looking at the pine straw below the bushes. I asked Curtis to get the gun and the hoe because there had to be a snake there. He did and as we walked up there the cardinals all flew but the bluebirds were so upset at the snake and involved in their mission that they totally forgot Curtis and continued to hover only about three feet from him as he killed the snake with the hoe. It turned out to be a copperhead, a very poisonous snake. So, the bluebirds did use good judgment in pointing it out and trying to attack it. It was really fascinating that the bluebirds momentarily lost all fear of Curtis and continued to flutter over the snake as Curtis chopped the snake with the hoe.

I was so tickled this morning (Wednesday 21) to see five martins circling the house and gourds and the TV antenna. They never did light anywhere and weren't even saying anything, but I was surprised to see them so late. I wonder if they were some of our martins and if so, where had they been? They were probably just some migrating birds that spotted our large martin complex and came down to check. The bluebirds, especially the juniors, enjoy exploring the martin gourds and houses this time of year, going in and out of all the holes. There were three bluebirds up on the martin wire when the martins kept flying over and the bluebirds got aggravated at the martins flying by so close and so fast.

I observed "Mrs. Blue" in the front yard the other morning seeking refuge in the front bluebird feeder in a 'hawk alert'. I just happened to be looking out the window when "Mrs. Blue" zoomed into the front bluebird feeder and at the same instant all the cardinals disappeared from the other feeders. I assume there must have been a hawk in the yard and one of the birds must have sounded the alarm call. "Mrs. Blue" hopped in the feeder and didn't eat a raisin right away. I guess that she was just seeking a safe place. I looked at the back yard and all the birds had disappeared there, too, as they always do during a hawk alert. I watched "Mrs. Blue" for over twenty minutes as she remained motionless in the feeder. Finally, I guess the hawk left, because a chickadee dropped down on the seed feeder. "Mrs. Blue" must have heard the chickadee because she came to life and ate two raisins and left the feeder since the danger was over.

We have gotten back the pictures (one roll color, and two rolls of b/w) and they weren't as good as we had hoped. The lighting wasn't great in some and none was quite as close as it appeared to be through the shutter. We still have one roll in the camera of color that hopefully will have some better shots, especially of the junior blues feeding the babies in the house on the fence. It has been

cloudy lately, so Curtis hasn't tried any more, but
will later. Will close for now.

Love,

T. and C.

19

August 28

Dear G. and R.

When you were here we were talking about our bluebird feeders and we did not finish; so, you asked me to write you about our feeders. Well, here goes.

Bluebird feeders provide bluebirds with extra food year-round. In hard winters, when ice and snow cover their natural food, bluebird feeders can make the difference. They can provide the nourishment necessary for bluebirds' survival. We leave the bluebird feeders up year-round and enjoy watching them being used every day. During the warm season the bluebirds still use them daily and even feed their babies from the feeders. When the babies are about ten days old we notice the bluebirds begin taking their babies raisins from the feeder.

When the babies fledge, it only takes a couple of weeks for them to figure out where their beloved raisins come from and they start sitting on top of the feeder begging for food. In another two or three weeks the babies are taught by their parents how to enter the feeders on their own. Bluebirds don't become too dependent on the feeders; they always eat more bugs than raisins daily, except when bugs are scarce. We enjoy watching the bluebirds use the feeders and knowing that we are helping them. An added benefit is that the feeders keep the bluebirds in the yard more often during the day and we get to see them more.

To get bluebirds to use the feeder we have found it best to start with some natural food. You need to pick some berries or fruit that bluebirds eat in nature, such as dogwood berries, holly berries, blueberries, pyracantha berries, pokeberries or other fruit being grown naturally in your yard or somewhere nearby. Then it is best to decide where you want to put the feeder in the yard. We think it is best to put it where it can be easily observed from inside your own house, but not too close to scare the birds. After you decide on a place, you will need to put down a post to place your feeder on, unless your spot is on an existing fence, or on the side of a tree that is in the open. A tree such as a pine would do, just so it isn't too shady or closed in.

It is best not to put up the feeder right away. First, mount a board to put the feeder on. On this board put the natural food and the food that you plan to use in your feeder (more on this later). Have patience because it usually takes a few days before the bluebirds discover their 'feeder board' and start their feast. After the bluebirds are eating both the natural food and the feeder food, then you can put the feeder on the feeder board with the foods inside of it.

It helps to have a "runway" at the two ends of the feeder where the bird entrance holes are. This gives them extra perching room and helps them find the entrance holes more easily. To get them started using the feeder place some of the food at the two ends close to the holes. You can skewer some of the food on toothpicks (gently, so they can remove it easily) and place it near the holes. Eventually stop putting food outside the feeder and have patience while the bluebirds learn to enter and exit the feeder. You can also stop using the natural food (berries or food that you pick) when the bluebirds start eating your chosen food.

Bluebirds usually adapt to and use the feeder sooner if it is put out for the first time in the winter or fall when the bug supply and natural foods are getting harder to find. But they will learn to use a feeder during spring and summer too; it just takes longer.

I must advise caution and fairly frequent observation when bluebirds, especially young bluebirds, are first learning to use the feeder. Sometimes they become confused after entering the feeder and forget how to get out and panic momentarily. We sometimes have to go outside and hand remove a young bluebird that has gotten scared and forgotten how to get out. So, if you have to be out of town when the bluebirds might be trying to learn to use the feeder, you should get a friend or neighbor to check the feeder about twice daily, or either take the feeder down and store it away until you return home; especially here, where days can reach the triple digits, a bluebird can get exhausted in the hot weather if it gets scared in the feeder and can't seem to locate an exit hole.

Our bluebird feeder has a sheet of plexiglass on each long side and cedar on the two short sides where the holes are located. We enjoy the two windows on the feeder because it gives us more visibility to watch the bluebirds feeding, but perhaps a feeder with only one window would be easier for a confused young bluebird to figure out more quickly. Bluebird feeders also should be nailed to their mounting platform or either tied down to prevent the wind from blowing the feeder off the mount.

We use raisins in our bluebird feeders and the bluebirds do adore them, but the raisins do have disadvantages. Some raisins are too big and we have to sort through them and cut some in half with the kitchen scissors so that the bluebirds will not choke on them. Also, in the summer time we have lots of hornets, wasps, and yellow jackets and, unfortunately, they often figure out the feeders and go inside to eat the sweet raisins. The bluebirds are smart and will not enter the feeder when the hornets, or related insects, are inside, so we have to go outside often (especially in hot, humid, moist weather, that the insects really love) and swat the insects and remove them from the feeders so that the bluebirds can use the feeders again. So, I don't know if I would particularly recommend raisins for your bluebird feeder, another reason being that the bluebirds like them so much that they may become spoiled on raisins and refuse to eat other foods that you might put in the feeder. We tried switching ours to peanut hearts, but the bluebirds were so fond of the raisins that we had little success. We do have some luck with pea sized pieces of beef suet (beef fat) in the winter time.

But we enjoy our bluebirds so much that we don't mind the trouble of cutting up the raisins and swatting the hornets and yellow jackets. Having a bluebird feeder does take patience and careful observation at times; but it is so rewarding to watch the bluebirds enjoying their tidbits. From dawn to dusk, watching the bluebirds eat a raisin of two always brings a smile to our faces and brightens up the moment for us year round.

Love,

T. and C.

20

Dear G. and R.

We survived our garage sale and hurricane Elena, so we had a busy weekend. We thought the group sale would get rained out Saturday but were glad when the storm stalled so we could have the sale and get it over with. We sold over $400 worth of things, so we did pretty well, but clothes did not sell well and we have a good bit of clothing left over. We got a couple of inches of rain from the hurricane, with only small limbs being blown down. We were fortunate, indeed!

We are getting ready to take off on our trip next week, so I've got to give mom lessons this week on which birds need tending to, when, and where. We were able to take down one hummingbird feeder this week and still have a one quart feeder up. I believe the hummers know when Labor Day comes because half of them seem to leave on Labor Day each year, but we still have at least a dozen hummers still with us.

Our youngest bluebirds, the three from the third brood in the front yard, still have their baby spots. Their chests haven't begun to turn rusty yet, they still look like juniors, fresh from the box. They

82

have all three learned to go in the front raisin feeder now and are so clever to watch. Quite often all three go in together. First, they gather outside the feeder and cuddle at the hole. They push and cuddle at each other against the feeder and the bracket holding the feeder. Then they slowly look up at the entrance hole and drop into the feeder one by one. All three eat from one to three raisins each, then they usually take a minute or two to cuddle in the feeder in the corner, one against the glass, one against the wood side, and one squeezed in the middle. Then they leave one by one and go off elsewhere to play. They are so funny when they play, too. They practice gathering building materials by pulling loose fibers off the cedar fance and gathering pine straw and then they practice mating by pecking each other on the back of the neck and then jumping on each other's backs.

Most of the juniors on the farm have started to change into their adult plumage now and are even downright strange looking, with their chests of a combination of spots and rust blotches and their heads have funny feather mixtures; some look white headed now and almost appear bald. But no matter how strange, they all are still adorable.

Many are going through a tail feather molt and have lost all or most all of their tail feathers. Our old-time favorites, "Mr. and Mrs. Blue" from the back yard, that have been with us as long as our house has been built, have both lost their tail feathers recently. "Mr. Blue's" have almost grown back in but "Mrs. Blue's" is real straggly and has quite a ways to grow. It doesn't take them long, thank goodness, and doesn't seem to affect their flight, as far as we can see.

We are getting so very many bluebirds everywhere on the farm now. I guess all the almost 280 babies and their parents are still here because we see them by the dozens everywhere, especially flying over the cut-over land. I believe I told you about it. It is about eighty acres that used to be one of my favorite spots. It was beautiful, with shady mixed woodlands, lots of holly and dogwoods, and a stream winding through it, until they clear-cut it about three years ago to plant pine trees. It is a very undesirable sight now but the only good thing that can be said about it is that the bluebirds enjoy it so much at this stage. The short pine trees are crowded with a jungle of briers and pokeberry plants. The jungle is too thick for us to walk through but the bluebirds fly over there and eat the pokeberries. We see flocks of forty to fifty flying there and when we walk over there to the edge we can usually see over 100 bluebirds. I suppose in another couple of years the pines will grow and crowd out the pokeberries and they will die off and then it won't be good for anything, not even pokeberries.

One of our Fox Squirrels has been gathering pine straw and grasses and taking them off into the top of a tall pine tree in the front yard. I don't know too much about squirrel nesting but I guess it is a mamma squirrel building a nest. She looks real funny with her mouth stuffed full, going across the fence trying to pull off some cedar fibers to add to her mouthful. I know the squirrels are glad that the bluebirds have finished nesting so they can move around the yard in peace.

The bluebirds, martins, and Barn Swallows used to give them (the squirrels) the devil, dive bombing them constantly until they would leave the yard.

I'll send you a postal card from out west and if we come to the September meeting of the Audubon Society, we'll give you a call before the meeting so we can arrange for the lens exchange that we were talking about. Take care. Hope plans for the big Reber family reunion are going smoothly.

Love,

T. and C.

21

September 6

Dear G. and R.

We made it back home after a vacation full of fun; hope you got our postcard. We were glad that our planned tour didn't work out; we had to leave Yellowstone Park early because of the snow, but we had already seen the whole park another year so we spent the extra nights in Cody and Thermopolis Hot Springs State Park, Wyoming. We enjoyed Denver, especially the large zoo and went to a play the night before we left, starring John Ritter (Three's a Crowd) and Beth Howland, among others. It was quite amusing.

Getting home we found it very dry. It hadn't rained the whole time we were gone, almost two weeks. But it rained the day we got home and also the next day, so we didn't have to water anything. The deer and rabbits had eaten up what was left in the garden and salvia in the yard, too. The hummingbirds seem to have all gone. I surely miss them!

We didn't get a newsletter for the September meeting, so we don't know if it was before or after we got home from our trip. We just were not sure when the meeting was to be. Our copy must have

PHOTO BY CURTIS DEW

EASTERN BLUEBIRD, MALE

PHOTO BY CURTIS DEW

EASTERN BLUEBIRD, FEMALE

PHOTO BY BRYAN SHANTZ

MOUNTAIN BLUEBIRD, MALE

PHOTO BY BRYAN SHANTZ

WESTERN BLUEBIRD, MALE

PHOTO BY REBER LAYTON

BLUEBIRD NEST IN BOX (EASTERN)

PHOTO BY GRAY LAYTON

BLUEBIRD NESTING BOX, SIDE OPEN, SHOWING
YOUNG ON NEST. HOUSE MOUNTED WITH FIRE
ANT GUARDS AND PREDATOR GUARD ON FRONT.

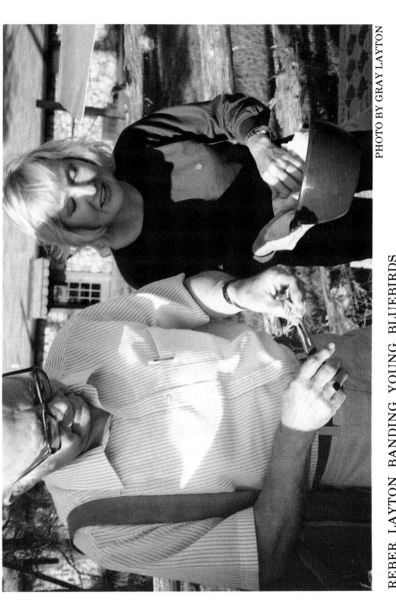

PHOTO BY GRAY LAYTON

REBER LAYTON BANDING YOUNG BLUEBIRDS FOR TINA DEW.

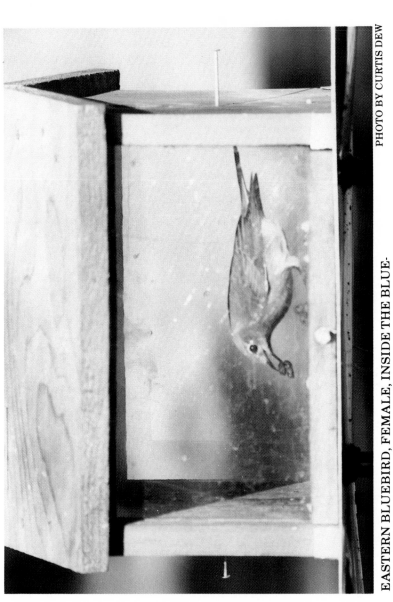

PHOTO BY CURTIS DEW

EASTERN BLUEBIRD, FEMALE, INSIDE THE BLUE-
BIRD FEEDER, VIEWED THROUGH PLEXIGLASS
SIDE, AS SHE PICKS UP RAISINS FOR HER YOUNG.

PHOTO BY CURTIS DEW

EASTERN BLUEBIRD, MALE, FEEDING HIS YOUNG
WITH FOOD FROM INSIDE THE FEEDER.

EASTERN BLUEBIRD, FEMALE, ABOUT LIFE SIZE

PHOTO BY CURTIS DEW

PHOTO BY REBER LAYTON

TYPICAL FIRE ANT HILL, A THREAT TO BLUEBIRDS,
NEXT TO POWER LINE POLE, AND ABOUT 12 FEET
FROM THE BLUEBIRD HOUSE IN THE REAR

PHOTO BY CURTIS DEW

A PAIR OF BLUEBIRDS EXAMINE A BLUEBIRD
HOUSE

PHOTO BY CURTIS DEW

EASTERN BLUEBIRD IN WINTER

PHOTO BY TINA AND CURTIS DEW

TINA AND CURTIS DEW IN THEIR FRONT YARD

Tina and Curtis Dew are young naturalists interested in all forms of wildlife conservation. They live on a beautiful 700 acre farm in Jasper County, Mississippi. The farm is couched between meandering streams which divide rolling countryside from wide prairie land. The farm is owned by Tina's parents, who specialize in cattle breeding.

Tina and Curtis built their own home completely by themselves, except for the house framing. Curtis is a very versatile household mechanic in every phase, a carry-over from his engineering background and his professional work as a jet engine mechanic for Dynalectron at the Key Air Base in Meridian. Tina, formerly a business management specialist, has recently stopped her work to pursue household engineering and bird watching intently.

A very limited hunting of deer only, by invitation only, is all that is permitted on the farm. The result is a haven for wildlife of all kinds.

PHOTO BY GRAY LAYTON

R.B. (REBER) LAYTON

R.B. (Reber) Layton, well known naturalist, has been active in wildlife conservation for many years and is the recipient of numerous awards for his conservation work, more recently with bluebirds. These awards include: the Jackson (MS) Audubon Society citation in recognition of outstanding contribution to the chapter by sponsoring the Jackson Bluebird Project; the Mississippi Wildlife Federation's State Governor's Award for the best statewide conservation effort of the year; and the North American Bluebird Society's coveted Nora Lane Award for national conservation efforts with bluebirds.

He is a charter and lifetime member of the North American Bluebird Society and serves on their Board of Directors. He organized and served as chairman of the first Mississippi Statewide Drive-in Bluebird conference and served as chairman of the Seventh International Conference of the North American Bluebird Society.

He is the author of two bird books, THE PURPLE MARTIN and 30 BIRDS THAT WILL BUILD IN BIRD HOUSES. He is now in his fifth year as chairman of the Jackson Bluebird Project, which has made and sold at cost over 30,000 bluebird houses across Mississippi as a part of the North American Bluebird Society's continental effort to bring back bluebirds.

PHOTO BY CURTIS DEW

EASTERN BLUEBIRD ENTERING THE BLUEBIRD FEEDER

gotten lost in the mail.

This cool weather is so nice. We had gotten used to cold/cool weather in the Rockies and were warm when we got home, but now it has gotten cooler and I hope it will stay this way.

This cool spell seems to have had a reverse effect on the birds somehow. It seems to have peaked their hormones just a bit, maybe a last chance for a little practice before winter sets in. The chickadees and the nuthatches have been going in their boxes the last day or two. The nuthatches in particular have been going in the front yard box often and bringing out bits of building material. We left their nest in the box since the eggs didn't hatch and the nest did not get dirty during the summer season.

The Pine Warblers, we call them chase birds, chase anything that flies, especially each other. This morning before Curtis had to leave for work we had a few minutes to sit out in the yard to watch the birds. We get up very early so we will have time to bird watch. Curtis almost fell out of his chair laughing at the pine warblers.They looked like mini-tornadoes as they chased each other round and round, almost running into us at times. Two even crashed into the kitchen window, they were so busy pursuing, but luckily were able to get off the ground and fly away when I went over to check on them.

As always, the bluebirds are putting on the best show. They have been singing up a storm, such beautiful music! But they also have been fighting a lot, especially the males. There was a pair on the ground in the front yard this morning, really battling it out. I watched them (two male bluebirds) for a minute and was just about to go outside and pull them apart when they broke apart on their own.

In the back they have been singing and playing in the martin gourds and the martin houses. At one time this morning there were eight bluebirds on the martin complex playing house all at once. "Mr. and Mrs." in the front were flittering and staying close together all morning, when he wasn't fighting with the others. She even lit on the ground during the big fight a few feet away from the scene and flittered. I guess she was a cheerleader for her husband. "Mr." followed her around, even lighting on top of the raisin feeder and singing while she was inside eating raisins. Later "Mrs.", of the same couple that had the front all summer, was in front of her house pulling fibers off the cedar rail, but she didn't take them into the house.

I believe some of the playing in the gourds in the back is in preparation for sleeping in them when the weather is cooler. We have had as many as three bluebirds sleeping in the martin gourds at once, that we are aware of. Maybe more have when we weren't watching. Curtis is going to clean out all of the gourds this weekend and remove the mud in the old martin nests. But out of the twenty gourds we are going to leave the mud nests in about five of them to see if the bluebirds prefer sleeping in the ones with nests or without nests. When the weather gets real cool, the mud nests would insulate and perhaps be warmer beds for the bluebirds, if they choose.

We have been enjoying a family of quail in the yard. All summer the adults (the couple) would come almost every day to eat under the bird feeders, but we never saw any babies until early September when we saw the couple in the blueberries with these tiny little knots (baby quail) following them. They were so darling! When we got back from vacation we wondered how the babies were and how much they had grown. In a couple of days we saw them in the back yard. They had grown a lot in the two weeks. They weren't quite adult size, still junior quail, but almost there. They are real cute still, but very shy, and fly if they see us, or run off rapidly. Their parents are tamer. I surely do hope they stay all year and will become tame. A flock of quail surely looks nice under the feeder.

We were so tickled to see Mountain Bluebirds in every state that we visited on our trip. At Yellowstone they were almost tame and also at Mammoth Hot Springs (at the north end of Montana), and at Old Faithful. Curtis took pictures and we hope that they will turn out to be good. We took lots of wildlife pictures also. They were taken with a telephoto lens and no tripod, so we aren't sure just how they will turn out. I will wait a few weeks in hope of catching a half-price sale for developing, since we have so many.

We also saw Barn Swallows everywhere, even flying by the windows of the grounded and take-off planes at the Denver Airport. We saw some young Barn Swallows perched in a tree near Heber, Utah, being fed by their parents.

Well, I had better start some supper cooking now. Hope that all is well and that we get to see one another soon.

Love,

T. and C.

22

October 30

Dear G. and R.

It seems that it will never stop raining. It has been raining almost non-stop since Saturday night and is predicted to rain at least through tomorrow. We must have gotten at least four inches of rain so far. I feel so sorry for all the birds outside. The rain and winds are so strong that it rains sideways and gets into the bird feeders and wets the seeds. Curtis said tonight that he was going to take the seed feeders down and put on bigger, more slanted roofs to help keep the seeds drier.

We are having trouble with our front yard "Mr. Blue", the same one that had three broods in the front house this summer. Saturday morning we got back from our after-breakfast walk and as soon as we entered the yard we heard the bluebirds in the front making what we call their 'panic' sound.

It is a warning call that usually means danger. Often a hawk or snake is nearby. The other birds in the yard always respond to the bluebirds' panic warning call by hiding. Even the big cardinals hide. We went right around to the front yard after

91

Curtis stopped to grab his gun in case we needed it. "Mr. Blue" was fussing frantically and "Mrs. Blue" was right beside him. We spent thirty minutes searching the bushes for snakes and the tree tops for killer hawks but we couldn't find a thing. "Mr. Blue" would hardly budge even though we walked right up on him. He kept up the constant alert calls. He even flew up into the gutter in front of our bedroom, flittering and fussing frantically.

We thought there must be a snake in the gutter, so Curtis climbed up on the roof and checked the gutters. No snake! "Mr. Blue" was still having a fit. He flew up on the antenna above Curtis' head, acting crazy. We finally gave up because we couldn't find anything. Curtis went to get the lawn mower to cut the grass. We figured that would scare off the intruder and calm down "Mr. Blue". I went inside and immediately heard a beating noise coming from the bedroom. I went over to see what it was and found "Mr. Blue" flying against the window, pecking away.

So that is what the big fuss was all about! "Mr. Blue" had gone crazy (only temporarily, we hope!) attacking the windows. Even when Curtis got the mower going, the racket still wasn't enough to stop "Mr. Blue" from his mission. I shut the curtains and that slowed him down, but it didn't stop him. He stood on the stone board and fussed, or would cling to the window, the metal divider between the top and bottom panes, pecking and fussing.

Sunday he kept it up off and on all day. Sometimes we would shoo him away and sometimes the rain would come down so hard that it would force him to stop.

Monday morning I went to Meridian so I shut the curtains in our bedroom to discourage him. When I got home around lunch time, I had a shocking experience to see the windows under the front porch. Curtis had cleaned them a week ago and they were then spotless. No more! Now they were filthy. "Mr. Blue" covered them with smears, wing prints and mess, covering the windows and the porch below with droppings. I had not shut the curtains because I didn't think he would come under the front porch.

We didn't know what caused this strange behavior, or just how to stop him. He acted normal all the year till now. He only attacks the windows in the front of the house (his territory). A week earlier (last week) when it was still real warm "Mr. and Mrs. Blue" (in the front) were doing lots of heavy courting and taking straw into their house. Both of them took about a dozen pieces of building materials and kept up the flittering for a couple of days until they gave up their house building for now. So, we are hoping that they will get involved in doing something else to take "Mr. Blue's" mind off this crazy new habit. I am getting tired of keeping all the curtains shut and having to turn on lights continually as I move from room to room.

I hope when the weather gets cooler he'll quit attacking the window bluebird. He is funny! He gets so mad that his throat moves constantly making fuss-alert sounds. He spreads his wings and his tail feathers as wide as they will go. It is quite a mystery. One day he is (or should I say several months) a normal bluebird that stays in the front yard from dawn to dusk looking at and ignoring the windows that he now feels compelled to attack.

At least "Mr. Blue" in the back yard still shows good sense! "Mr. Blue" has spent the better part of the last three days staying under the woodshed out of the hurricane winds and torrential rains. He comes out when the weather slackens up to go into his raisin feeder for a fill-up and then he grabs a few quick bugs and back to his shed, where it is dry.

We went to Hattiesburg a couple of days ago to visit Larry and Terry Gates and to see their new home and went on a picnic and bird watching with them and the Hattiesburg Audubon Society. We were thrilled to see a male Rose-breasted Grosbeak.

If the weather clears up, we are planning on going to the Gulf Coast this weekend to the meeting of the Mississippi Ornithological Society gathering. We always enjoy their meeting and we haven't been to the coast in over five years. But we don't know much about the coast line shore birds. I don't know one gull from another, or a gull from a tern.

We had a Brown-headed Nuthatch that died a few days ago. It was real sad! We watched him for over a week and knew that he was sick, but by the time he was so sick that we could pick him up, it was too late to save him. I don't know if we could have helped him anyway. We have a book that tells about ailments and it sounded like he had an intestinal infection and needed anti-biotics.

For over a week we noticed him moving slowly, for a nuthatch, and he would sleep during the day on the feeder, the tree, or even the ground. He was real fat and puffed up from being sick. When he died, we examined him for possible ticks or injuries and could not find anything. His eye lids had crusty tears in the corners. It was so sad! I really loved the little nuthatch! Now, there seems to be another that is looking puffy and slow. I surely do hope that he gets better and that we aren't going to have another fatality. I am going to talk to Jerry Jackson about it when we see him.

We were surprised and glad to see an osprey at our house (flying over the big lake) last Sunday. I guess he was migrating and the weather was bad, so he stopped over for a few hours. The dumb crows kept chasing him away and the bluebirds sounded the warning call. They had never seen an osprey before and they were afraid. They didn't know that he was a fish eater.

An encouraging sign - lately we've seen bluebirds in Meridian on several occasions. I surely hope they can survive; but for every bluebird in town (Meridian), there must be hundreds of House Sparrows.

We haven't taken any more pictures of birds lately. The bluebirds have been unpredictable as far as bathing and feeding (raisins) schedules, and the weather has been bad. I guess this time of the year the sun doesn't shine a lot and when it does, it doesn't shine on the bird bath or the feeders for very long. Now the days are so short. Curtis just hates the time change because it is almost dark when he gets home from work. We got our vacation pictures back and they were pretty good. The color prints of the junior bluebirds feeding the babies were mixed. A couple with the sun just right were good and the others without bright sunlight weren't. We have learned that you have to have a good sunlight for good bird pictures. We will show them to you when we get together and then you can see what you think of them. I wish we could get a picture of "Mr. Crazy" attacking the window, but it would probably be blurred. Curtis says that if "Mr. Blue" doesn't stop messing up the windows soon, he will catch him and spray Windex on his wings so he can clean the windows instead of making a mess of them, or either give "Mr. Blue" a bottle of Windex and a roll of paper towels and tell him to clean up when he gets through playing.

Well, I had better sign off and get some work done. Hope we can get together soon. If you all feel like a ride, come see us some weekend. I'll fix lunch and we will look at bluebirds. Take care and write when you recover from all the genealogy festivities.

Love,

T. and C.

23

Dear G. and R.

It is a cool Tuesday and I hope it stays cool. Maybe the yellow jackets will hibernate or die if the weather stays cool enough and we'll (we and the bluebirds) rest easier again. Then the bluebirds will be able to eat more raisins. "Mr. Blue" in the front is still attacking the windows on a daily basis. It is funny, aggravating, and sad to watch him; especially when the weather is warm it is saddening to see him work so hard at such a useless chore. He just wears himself out if we don't chase him away. He'll keep it up until he is panting with his beak open and breathing hard, and his feathers will be all messed up from colliding with the windows.

He is also expanding his window territory. He started with the bedroom double front windows and then went to the side windows. Next he started coming under the front porch and attacking the pair of double windows. He'll either perch on the hangers that hold the hummingbird feeders between attacks or he'll just hop to the porch floor. He is real funny sometimes. He'll be on the fence forty feet away from the porch and he'll just fly straight into the porch, real low, and land under the porch chair. Then he'll hop around on the porch for a few minutes like a robin and if I don't shoo him away, he'll fly up and start pecking the windows.

Sometimes when I shoo him he'll just fly under the carport until I leave the window area. Then he'll come back, pecking and fussing. It is amazing to see him hopping around on the front porch. We've never had a bluebird to do that. He often gets bugs off the porch and eats them, and we appreciate that.

Yesterday morning when I came back from my walk, I stopped as I entered the yard because I heard the bluebird alert fuss sound. I was really surprised when I saw FYMB (front yard "Mr. Blue") pecking at the back long window and three other bluebirds (I assume BYMB, back yard "Mr. Blue", and his wife and FYMB's wife also - four bluebirds total) were perched on the edge of the gutter looking down at him, trying to figure out what he was fussing and alerting about.

I could hardly believe that he had come out of his territory to attack a back window and the BYMB let him do it! I know that they are supposed to be basically territorial during nesting season and not during the winter season, but our yard ones seem to be territorial to a degree year round. I came into the yard and I played a trick on FYMB and got him to leave the back window alone for a little while. We had bought a 'bird saver', a silhouette of a hawk, to try to keep so many birds from running into the windows and getting killed. We hadn't put it up yet so when "Mr. Blue" kept at the back windows, I taped it to the pane when he was perched on the wire with his back turned. Then I stood still and waited. He doesn't see us, or care if we watch, provided we are still. After only a couple of minutes he was back and headed for the pane with the taped bird on it. He got within about two feet and a look of surprise and confusion came over his face (if one can really determine this). He turned around and flew away and just looked and looked at the window.

He came over again for a closer look a couple more times but he didn't peck that window any more all day. Curtis immediately ran off some more hawk pictures and I cut them out. I plan to tape them in all of the windows and see if that will cure him. I have my fingers crossed, though.

We enjoy watching some of our bluebirds go to bed. At least four or five are sleeping in the little pine tree right opposite our yard cattle gap. We hung these black plastic flower pots, two of them, in a pine tree a year ago and the bluebirds sleep in them, two or more bluebirds per pot. Curtis hung them with fine wire from the branches but they are pretty concealed with pine boughs partially covering the tops of the pots. As the bluebirds pile in at night the pots rock back and forth and if you are in the yard and all is quiet, you can hear them shuffling around and making little noises in the pots. They are so funny and precious!

We haven't received our Jackson Audubon Society's news letter yet, but if we do, we will give you a call to see if you are coming so we can bring our pictures that you haven't seen.

We are planning to go to New Orleans for Thanksgiving, if the latest hurricane doesn't mess up everything.

We have lots of goldfinches, juncos, and Chipping Sparrows at our feeders already. I was thrilled yesterday to see a couple of Pine Siskins drinking at the front bird bath. We have had a bumper crop of pecans after a couple of years that were slow producers, but the only problem is that half of them are bad. We still have to pick up and crack bad ones and try to cull them as we pick them out. For the last two or three weeks we have picked out pecans about every night. We pour the hulls and bad ones in the back yard under the rail fence. The wrens and juncos pick through them and eat a little and the Fox Squirrels tried them but returned quickly to eat spilled sunflower seeds beneath the feeders. I figured (wrongly) that the squirrels would go for the pecans in a big way and leave the ground beneath the feeders in peace for the scratching ground feeding birds - wrong, wrong, wrong!

Well, if I close now, I can put this in today's mail, maybe. Hope to see you all, if we come to Jackson. If not, have a Happy Thanksgiving!

Love,

T. and C.

24

Dear G. and R.

We really enjoyed our visit with you all Saturday so much and are looking forward to you all coming to visit us. Your lovely home is so relaxing, and we loved the tile porch floor of the covered patio, with the hand painted tiles that Gray made and put there. And thanks so much for the hand painted and fired wild turkey original. It is just beautiful! We treasure it so much!

Curtis tried to get some bluebird pictures Sunday afternoon but the bluebirds weren't in a cooperative mood. We're hoping for a sunny weekend coming up and more luck with the subject. Curtis doesn't get home till 4:30 during the week and the sun is too low by then. He'll try hard this weekend.

This cold weather has all of the birds eating 'tons of food'. We must have at least 100 Purple Finches, 150 Chipping Sparrows, seventy juncos, forty goldfinches, twenty Pine Siskins, thirty cardinals, twenty Pine Warblers, thirty Yellow-rump Warblers, twenty assorted woodpeckers (Red-bellied, Downy, flicker, sapsucker), ten chickadees, five Brown-headed Nuthatches, two Song Sparrows (hope I don't forget any) at our yard feeders now and at least ten bluebirds eating over 200 raisins per day.

Well, I'll close now so I can get this in today's mail. Come see us whenever you can. We'd love to have you visit, and I'd love to fix lunch for us. I love cooking, the only household job I really like, and especially for company. So, let us fix something when you all come. I'll keep it simple, but it is fun for me. Take care and we'll be looking forward to seeing you all.

Love,

T. and C.

25

Dear G. and R.

These warm winter days are inspiring the blue-birds to begin singing before daybreak. We can hear our yard bluebirds sweet songs while it is still dark outside. They are examining their houses and flittering their wings as they practice their courting.

In the late afternoon they perform aerial tricks as they fly from their perches to catch the flying bugs; they are as graceful as the phoebes, as they make aerial loop-the-loops (like stunt airplanes) before landing. Watching them closely with the binoculars reveals they are eating quite a few mosquitoes. It doesn't seem that such a tiny insect would be worth the effort they put forth to get it, but it apparently does satisfy them.

Temperatures surpassed the sixties today, and less than a week ago we had the coldest weather of all winter, with the wind chill factor near zero. Even our bird bath heater needed some help as the baths froze around the edges away from the heaters. I had to take out pans of warm water to help thaw out all of them. All the birds were so grateful for the heated baths on that frigid day.

Many waded in the steaming water, probably because it felt warm compared to the windy weather in the teens.

As cold as that day was it didn't stop our crazy front yard "Mr. Blue" from his window pecking mission. He even started up before 8 a.m. while it was still below twenty degrees with twenty mile per hour winds! It is incredible that he would waste that much energy on such a cold day. All the other bluebirds were wisely conserving body heat by fluffing out their feathers and not moving around much. Most were sitting in spots where the north wind was blocked off by a nearby tree, etc. There is one male in the backyard that we laugh at, but he is really smart. You know that we have an outside wood burning heater. This male has taken full advantage of it. The outside of the heater is metal and stays slightly warm to the touch. This male spends much time, especially on cold mornings, perched on the warm heater. When he wants to change positions on his warm perch, he doesn't fly from front to back of the heater, he hops across. He must have poor circulation in his toes and have cold feet because he really loves his warm perch. Also, he seems to find more insects around the heater. I guess bugs are smart enough to seek out warm places also.

I have to tell you more about our crazy "Mr. Blue" from the front yard. As before mentioned, he is still pecking on windows all over the house and also pecks the bluebird feeders' plexiglass windows. He is the same one that last summer arrived just in time to rescue "Mrs. Blue" from her predicament. She (to refresh your memory) had mated with her father, from the summer of a year ago; but her father and mother were both still together and raising broods in the back yard. "Mr. Blue" found himself with two wives and two sets of babies to feed, so, when forced to choose, abandoned his daughter and her family in the front yard when it got too much for him to handle. He then went back to his wife in the back yard and let his daughter down with hungry mouths to feed. So, crazy "Mr. Blue" showed up with his rough coat and finally adopted the babies after "Mrs. Blue" was instantly infatuated with him. After learning to use the raisin feeder and the bath, his plumage gradually improved until his blue, rust, and white smoothed out and he became handsome enough to equal any male. After his adopted babies met disaster from a snake, he and "Mrs." regrouped and recovered and raised two more broods in the front yard. The clashes between the two pairs actually increased somewhat after breeding season was over. Their territories are so close together and overlap so they have remained territorial year round to a degree.

Anyway, in the fall, front yard "Mr. Blue" just 'flipped out'. He started attacking windows and making the alert-panic calls frequently during the day, and for no reason. Maybe his history is what caused him to have a mental breakdown. "Mrs. Blue", his wife, has remained faithful all through this and adores him so, no matter how much abuse he subjects her to. Since he has started pecking the bluebird feeder, he has also prevented "Mrs. Blue" from entering the feeder whenever she chose to do so. If she goes into the feeder and he doesn't want her to, he goes in right behind her and pecks at her. She immediately flees, exiting the feeder as fast as possible, not even slowing down long enough to pick up a raisin. Last week, one morning, I looked out the window just in time to see her go into the feeder. She must not have known that "Mr. Blue" was on his way, because as she picked up a raisin in the corner, he zoomed in and cornered her. I couldn't believe my eyes as he viciously attacked her. Hating to interfere, I watched for over a minute but couldn't stand it any more and feared that he might kill her. I ran outside and could hear her cries as I ran toward the feeder. I lifted the top and shouted at him but he paid me no attention, just continuing to peck her furiously. Finally, I pulled them apart and held her in one hand and him in the other hand. I let them both free but, in hindsight, I wish that I would have kept him and spanked his tail or at least given him a good talking to. A few days later we noticed that Mrs. Blue had a fresh injury on her stomach. I have no proof but I believe that "Mr. Blue" must have been responsible for it. I do wish I knew how to cure this mental problem of his!

Yesterday a male Purple Finch lit on the bluebird feeder and "Mr. Blue" sailed in, knocked him off, and pinned the finch to the ground, pecking constantly until I beat on the window and distracted him long enough for the finch to escape. Now that the weather is warming, the honey bees are entering the feeders to eat raisins. "Mr. Blue" snaps at them but I haven't seen him eat one yet.

We enjoyed our visit with you all Tuesday! The drinks and snacks in your lovely home, in front of the roaring fire, while watching the large assortment of birds outside your patio, was delightful. The seafood dinner was absolutely delicious and we thank you for inviting us. We hope you all will come to visit us soon so we can try to repay your kind hospitality.

After our garden quit yielding in the fall, Curtis plowed it under to kill the weeds. Then he took half a dozen old bean poles and stuck them into the soft ground until we get ready to use the garden again and then he can easily remove the poles. The bluebirds love them and perch out there regularly. They also help us by removing insects from the garden.

I got a letter from Dr. Field of Centerville, MS (from the bluebird conference). He had bought a bluebird feeder from us and wrote to tell me that his bluebirds finally were using it. They were eating dogwood berries but not raisins. I am going to write him and tell him that he is probably lucky, because the raisins are more trouble because the bees and yellow jackets start coming to the feeders.

None of our winter birds have left, even though it is practically February. This morning I was scanning the flock under the back feeder for any unusual species when I noticed one of the Pine Siskins had a band on its leg. The sun was shining and I just happened to catch the glare with my binoculars as the little piney moved. It is always amazing to see a banded bird and wonder where it came from and who banded it and where.

I better sign off before I have to put two stamps on this envelope. Again, thanks so much for the unexpected treat Tuesday. We always enjoy visiting with you all so much! I told Curtis I wish I could adopt you all and bring you both home with us! Come visit whenever you can. The weekend is supposed to be warm and pretty, I'm hoping not cloudy, so Curtis can try to get some bluebird shots. Take care.

Love,

T. and C.

HOW TO ATTRACT
AND
RAISE BLUEBIRDS

ABOUT BLUEBIRDS

Once you have seen the true Eastern Bluebird, you will never mistake it again. With a coat of the purest, richest and most gorgeous blue on its back, wings, and tail, it simply cannot have a mistaken identity. Its peach to rusty brown colored breast, followed by a soft white under its rump completes its beauty. The female is less colorful.

The early Plymouth Colony settlers quickly learned to welcome this friendly, cheerful songster, which reminded them of their beloved English "Robin Redbreast". They quickly named it the "Blue Robin", a name that is still attached to it by some "old timers".

The great New England writer, Henry David Thoreau, said that the bluebird carried the blue of heaven on its back and the rich brown of the freshly turned earth on its breast. An ample description of this beautiful bird! One quickly learns to love it not only for its handsome appearance, but for its sweet, melodious tones of voice. Especially is this true in early spring when the male begins to convince his mate to take up abode in the site that he has found. He carols his sweetest, most seductive notes day after day in his attempted attraction. When finally successful, he displays his charms further by spreading his tail feathers, lowering his half-opened wings and warbling soft undertones to secure her favor. Finally, when successful with his wooing techniques, he leads her to the selected nesting site, looks in, and tries to entice her to venture inside. That nesting site could be yours, if you have a nesting box ready for the male bluebird to select.

THE BLUEBIRD SUCCESS STORY

Until very recently, the American bluebird population was dangerously on the decline. It is true that some twenty-five to fifty years ago, bluebirds had no trouble reproducing and maintaining their population. Since they will nest only in cavities and prefer open areas, they used to adopt deserted woodpecker holes in fence posts, telephone and light poles, apple trees, and the like, as their usual homes.

When human beings started to replace the natural wooden poles with chemically treated ones or poles of metal and concrete, the woodpeckers no longer used them and so no longer left the usual nesting holes for bluebirds to use. Likewise, when wooden fence posts were replaced with metal and concrete, woodpeckers found it necessary to retreat from the open spaces back into the woods, where bluebirds will not live. As a result there were fewer and fewer cavities for bluebirds to nest in, and fewer and fewer bluebirds were born each year. The use of dangerous pesticides, before they were banned, played its part in decreasing the bluebird population.

Now, however, nature lovers have come to the bluebirds' rescue. They have learned that bluebirds will nest in a man made house erected only three to five feet above the ground. The deserted woodpecker hole rapidly is being replaced by the new man-made wooden box. Wildlife organizations and individuals throughout the United States, Canada and Bermuda are joining in the effort to save the bluebird from extinction, and a great success story has already begun.

WHERE BLUEBIRDS LIVE

The Bluebirds range across the United States, Canada and Bermuda from the Atlantic Ocean to the Pacific Ocean. The Rocky Mountains are the home of the Mountain Bluebird, and west of the Rockies, that of the Western Bluebird; while the largest territory, from the Rockies to the Atlantic Ocean, is the domain of the Eastern Bluebird. Of course, these territorial divisions are not strictly observed, and there are even instances of cross-breeding.

Each of the three species has a distinct color pattern. The Eastern Bluebird, about the size of the well known House Sparrow, wears a beautiful rusty brown breast and a blue back, head, and tail. It can be seen in both winter and summer in the lower states, since it is a yearlong resident there. The Mountain Bluebird wears a solid blue and is slightly larger than the Eastern Bluebird; while the Western Bluebird carries the blue color across the front with both brown and blue across the back. Bluebirds can be seen in largest numbers during the winter months, particularly in the southern states, since they, like many other bird species, band together for protection and feeding during the cold weather, pairing off and becoming territorial in spring for nesting and raising their young.

Unfortunately bluebirds are not easily attracted to cities. They prefer outlying areas, small towns, and rural settings. Through combining our efforts to provide housing for bluebirds, they may some day move into our cities — after they are more plentiful. Doves have shown us an example of this moving. Dwellers in town and city suburbs have, for the past several years, enjoyed looking up to see doves sitting together on light wires, seeking bird-seed scattered on the ground under a feeder-pole, and hearing the soft cooing voices of these beautiful birds. Perhaps bluebirds will "come in" also!

FOOD AND HOUSING
FOR THE BLUEBIRDS

What Bluebirds Eat

There is not much that bluebird lovers can do to provide nice, juicy insects for their little friends to eat! But two very effective means exist to supplement their vegetable diet. One is to plant trees and shrubs whose natural fruits and berries are especially loved by the bluebirds. The other is artificial feeding by human beings in a sheltered feeding station. Both of these are recommended ways to attract and provide for your bluebirds.

How to Provide Natural Fruits and Berries for Bluebirds

Many geographical areas within the bluebird's winter range do not have sufficient quantities of fruit producing trees and shrubs that hold their fruit through the winter months. It is very helpful when bluebird lovers plant fruit producers to help the bluebirds sustain life through the winter season.

Likewise, summer and autumn fruit producers can play an important part in attracting and holding bluebirds within your territory.

George N. Grant, an active bluebird enthusiast has developed a list of recommended plantings for winter fruits and another list for summer and autumn fruit bearing, *SIALIA* 9(1):68, which are shown in the following tables.

Table 1. Trees and shrubs having high wildlife values, most of which hold their fruit well into the winter season.

Common Name	Botanical Name
Red Chokeberry	Aronia arbutifolia
Spicebush	Benzoin aestivale
Bittersweet	Celastrus scandens
Hackberry	Celtis occidentalis
Flowering Dogwood	Cornus florida
Small-leaved Cotoneaster	Cotoneaster microphylla
Washington Hawthorn	Crataegus phaenopyrum
Blackthorn	Crataegus tomentosa
Inkberry, Pokeweed	Ilex glabra
Smooth Winterberry	Ilex laevigata
American Holly	Ilex opaca
Black Alder	Ilex verticillata
Western Red Cedar	Juniperus scopulorum
Red Cedar	Juniperus virginiana
Privet	Ligustrum vulgare
Amur Honeysuckle	Lonicera maacki
Moonseed	Menispermum canadense
Bayberry	Myrica carolinesis
Sour Gum	Nyssa sylvatica
Virginia Creeper	Parthenocissus quinquefolia

Pyracantha	Pyracantha sp.
Small Sumac	Rhus copallina
Smooth Sumac	Rhus glabra
Staghorn Sumac	Rhus typhina
Multiflora Rose	Rosa multiflora
Mountain Ash	Sorbus americana
Coralberry	Symphoricarpos orbiculatus
High-bush Cranberry	Viburnum opulus
Blackhaw	Viburnum prunifolium

Table 2. Trees and shrubs having high wildlife values, most of which carry fruit in summer and autumn. Many species are valued for human consumption.

Common Name	Botanical Name
American Elderberry	Sambucus canadensis
Scarlet Elderberry	Sambucus pubens
Service Berry	Amelanchier sp.
Tatarian Honeysuckle	Lonicera tatarica
Wild Grape	Vitis sp.
European Mountain Ash	Sorbus aucuparia
Flowering Crab	Malus sp.
Common Buckthorn	Rhamnus cathartica
Mapleleaf Viburnum	Viburnum acerifolium
Hobblebush	Viburnum alnifolium
Nannyberry	Viburnum lentago
Arrow Wood	Viburnum dentatum
Witherod	Viburnum cassinoides
Siebold Viburnum	Viburnum sieboldi

Alternate-leaf Dogwood	Cornus alternifolia
Silky Dogwood	Cornus amomum
Gray Dogwood	Cornus racemosa
Roundleaf Dogwood	Cornus rugusa
Red-osier Dogwood	Cornus stolonifera
Cornelian Cherry	Cornus mas
Kousa Dogwood	Cornus kousa
Common Snowberry	Symphoricarpos albus
Lowbush Blueberry	Vaccinium angustifolium
Highbush Blueberry	Vaccinium corymbosum
Black Huckleberry	Gaylussacia baccata
Wild Blackberry	Rubus allegheniensis
Japanese Barberry	Berberis thunbergi
Pin Cherry	Prunus pensylvanica
Common Chokeberry	Prunus virginiana
Black Cherry	Prunus serotina
Red Mulberry	Morus ruba
White Mulberry	Morus alba
Russian Olive	Elaeagnus angustifolia
Russian Olive	Elaeagnus angustifolia
Autumn Olive	Elaeagnus umbellata
Asiatic Sweetleaf	Symplocos paniculata
Greenbrier	Smilax sp.

The following chart of hardiness zones, developed by the U.S. Agricultural Research Service of the U.S. Department of Agriculture, and its following Key charts to usage by hardiness zones is provided by George Grant *SIALIA* 3(1) 27-31. "It was designed", said Grant, "to help those who would like to start their own wildlife planting program, utilizing basically native and wild plantings."

The hardiness zones 1-10 are based on the average annual minimum temperature for each zone and divide the United States and Canada into areas where specific plants are winter hardy. Many factors such as altitude, length of growing season, exposure, moisture, soil types, etc. can create variations within zones, but adhering to your specific zone will generally give you the best results.

ZONE 1	BELOW -50^0
ZONE 2	-50^0 TO -40^0
ZONE 3	-40^0 TO -30^0
ZONE 4	-30^0 TO -20^0
ZONE 5	-20^0 TO -10^0
ZONE 6	-10^0 TO 0^0
ZONE 7	0^0 TO 10^0
ZONE 8	10^0 TO 20^0
ZONE 9	20^0 TO 30^0
ZONE 10	30^0 TO 40^0

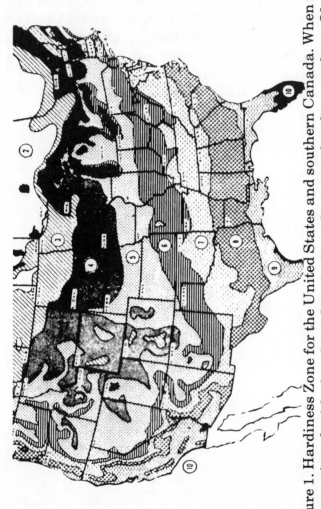

Figure 1. Hardiness Zone for the United States and southern Canada. When no zones are mentioned with the plant description, plants are hardy anywhere. If a zone is given, it indicates that plants are hardy within the zone and in all areas south of it. (Courtesy U.S. Dept. of Agriculture)

KEY

X - Depends on Species

Tree - Shrub - Vine	T - S - V
Size	A - 1-3'; B - 3-6'; C - 6-10'; D - 10-15'; E - 15-20'; F - 20-30'; G - 30-50'; H - 50-80'; I over 80'
Native - Escaped - Cultivated	N - Native; E - Escaped form Cultivation; C - Cultivated
Hardiness Zone	Zones 1-10
Deciduous or Evergreen	D or E
Landscape Value	E - Excellent; G - Good; N - Naturalizing
Specimen or Mass	S or M or E - Either
Flower Display	E - Excellent; F - Fair; P - Poor
Flower Color	White; Red; Pink; Yellow; Greenish
Fruit Color	Bk - Black; B - Blue; R - Red; O - Orange; P - Purple; W - White
Fruit Size	A=1/8"; B=1/4"; C=3/8"; D=1/2"; E=5/8" or larger
Fruit Display	E - Excellent; G - Good; P - Poor
Fruiting Period	Jan = 1; Dec = 12. Ex. 9-3 = Sept to Mar
Fall Foliage	E - Excellent G - Good; N - Not Effective
Light Requirement	1 - Full Sun; 2 - Part Sun; 3 - Shade
Soil Requirement	A - Wet; B - Normal Garden; C - Dry; D - Dry Poor
Soil pH	A - Acid; B - Mildly Acid; C - Mildly Alkaline
Plant Sex	A - M+F on Separate Plants; B - M+F on Same Plant; C - Either of the Above
Plant Source	A - Most Nurseries; B - Some Nurseries; C - Specialized Nurseries; D - Dig from Wild
Method of Transplanting	A - Dormant with Soil Ball; B - Dormant with Bare Roots when Small; D - Difficult
Propogation	A - Seeds; B - Stem Cuttings; C - Root Cuttings; D - Suckers; E - Difficult; Refer to Referecence
Bluebird Use	A - Preferred; B - Limited; C - Minimal
Wildlife Value	E - Excellent; G - Good; F - Fair; P - Poor
Winter Survival Food	E - Excellent; G - Good; P - Poor

	Tree, Shrub, Vine	Size	Native, Escaped Cultivated	Hardiness Zone	Deciduous or Evergreen	Landscape Value	Specimen or Mass	Flower Display	Flower Color	Fruit Color	Fruit Size	Fruit Display	Fruiting Period	Fall Foliage	Light Requirement	Soil Requirement	Soil pH	Plant Sex	Plant Source	Method of Transplanting	Propagation	Bluebird Use	Wildlife Value	Winter Survival Food
American Elderberry	S	C	N	4	D	G	E	E	W	P/BK	A	G	8-10	N	2	AB	B	B	BCD	B	ABD	A	E	P
Scarlet Elderberry	S	C	N	4	D	G	E	E	W	R	A	E	6-9	N	1.2.3	BC	BC	B	CD	B	ABD	B	G	P
Serviceberry	T	FG	N	3-5X	D	E	S	E	W	R	A	G	6-8	N	1.2	BC	BC	B	BCD	AC	A	B	E	P
Tatarian Honeysuckle	S	C	E	4	D	G	E	F	WP	P	C	G	6-10	N	1.2	BC	BC	B	A	B	A	B	G	P
Wild Grape	V	FG	N	3-6X	D	N	E	P	G	BBK	BC XD	P	9-3	N	1.2	B	BC	A	D	B	A	A	E	E
Flowering Crab	T	X	E	X	D	E	S	E	X	X	CDE	G	X	N	1	B	BC	B	A	B	E	B	E	X
Common Buckthorn	ST	DE	E	2	D	N	S	P	G	BK	BC	G	9-1	N	1.2	BC	BC	A	CD	B	A	C	F	G
Mapleleaf Viburnum	S	B	N	4	D	N	M	F	W	P/BK	B	G	9-3	N	2.3	AB	BC	B	CD	B	AD	B	F	G
Highbush Cranberry	S	CD	N	2	D	E	E	E	R	R	C	E	9-3	N	2	AB	AB	B	BCD	B	ABC	B	F	E

122

Plant	Tree, Shrub, Vine	Size	Native, Escaped, Cultivated	Hardiness Zone	Deciduous or Evergreen	Landscape Value	Specimen or Mass	Flower Display	Flower Color	Fruit Color	Fruit Size	Fruit Display	Fruiting Period	Fall Foliage	Light Requirement	Soil Requirement	Soil pH	Plant Sex	Plant Source	Method of Transplanting	Propagation	Bluebird Use	Wildlife Value	Winter Survival Food
Hobblebush	S	BC	N	4	D	N	E	E	W	RP	C	E	8-10	G	2,3	B	B	B	CD	B	AD	C	F	P
Nannyberry	ST	DE	N	2	D	G	S	E	W	B/BK	D	G	9-2	G	1,2	ABC	BC	B	CD	AB	A	B	F	G
Southern Arrowwood	S	CD	N	3	D	E	E	F	W	B	B	E	8-10	E	1,2	AB	BC	B	BCD	AB	A	B	G	P
Witherod	S	C	N	3	D	E	E	E	W	B·BK	B	E	9-12	G	1,2	B	BC	B	CD	AB	S	B	G	P
Alternate-leaf Dogwood Cornus alternifolia	ST	EF	N	4	D	E	S	F	W	B·BK	B	G	8-9	G	1,2	B	B	B	CD	FB	A	A	E	P
Silky Dogwood	S	C	N	5	D	G	E	F	W	BW	B	G	9-10	N	1,2	AB	B	B	CD	AB	A	A	E	P
Gray Dogwood	S	BC	N	4	D	E	E	F	W	W	B	E	9-12	G	1,2	BC	BC	B	CD	AB	A	A	E	P
Red-osier Dogwood	S	BC	N	2	D	E	M	F	W	W	B	G	7-10	N	1,2	ABC	BC	B	BCD	AB	AB	A	E	P
Cornelian cherry	T	E	C	4	D	E	S	E	Y	R	E	G	7-8	N	1,2	B	BC	B	B	A	E	B	G	P
Kousa Dogwood	T	E	C	5	D	E	S	E	W	R	E	G	9-10	E	1	B	AB	B	B	A	A	B	E	P

123

Common Snowberry	S	B	N	4	D	N	M	P	W	W	C-E	E	8-11	N	1,2,3	BCD	BC	B	A	AB	BD	C	F	P
Highbush Blueberry *Vaccinium corymbosum*	S	C	N	4	D	E	S	P	W	B	BC	E	8-9	E	1,2	B	A	B	AD	A	A	A	E	P
Wild Blackberry	S	B	N	4	D	N	M	F	W	BK	E	G	7-9	N	1,2	B	BC	B	A	AD	AB	B	B	P
Japanese Barberry	S	B	E	5	D	E	E	P	Y	R	D	E	8-3	N	1	BC	BC	B	A	AB	AB	C	G	E
Pin Cherry	T	EF	N	2	D	G	E	E	W	R	B	E	7-9	N	1	BCD	BC	B	CD	AB	A	A	E	P
Common Chokecherry	T	DE	N	2	D	N	S	E	W	RBK	C	G	7-10	N	1	BC	BC	B	CD	AB	A	A	E	P
Black Cherry	T	H	N	4	D	N	S	F	W	P	C	G	8-9	N	1,2	B	BC	B	CD	AB	A	A	E	P
Red Mulberry	T	G	N	5	D	E	S	P	G	RP	D	G	7-9	N	1	B	B	C	CD	AB	A	A	E	P
White Mulberry	T	G	E	4	D	G	S	P	G	WP	D	G	7-9	N	1	BC	BC	C	A	AB	AB	A	E	P
Russian Olive	TS	E	E	2	D	E	E	P	Y	Y	D	G	8-3	N	1	BC	BC	B	A	AB	AB	A	E	E
Autumn Olive	S	D	E	4	D	G	E	P	Y	R	C	E	9-11	N	1	BC	BC	B	A	AB	A	B	E	P
Greenbrier	V	F	N	X	D	N	E	P	G	B/BK	B	P	9-3	N	1,2	B	BC	B	D	AB	A	B	E	E

124

How to Build a Sheltered Bluebird Feeder

One of the greatest joys of raising wild birds is to watch them at close range. There is no more effective way to get bluebirds near your window than a bird feeder, as the previous letters have made so clear. The illustrated plan which follows shows how to construct a successful bluebird feeder.

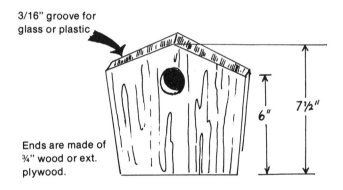

3/16" groove for glass or plastic

Ends are made of ¾" wood or ext. plywood.

6"

7½"

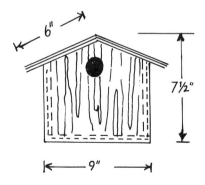

6"

7½"

9"

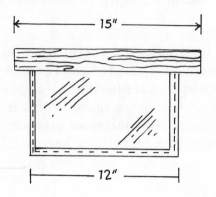

15"

12"

Top is made of
¼" or heavier
ext. plywood or
lumber. One
side is hinged.

Floor is made of
½" ext. plywood
or ¾" lumber.

This type of feeder was introduced to bluebirders
by Vera Gourley in *SIALIA* 1(1):144-145. It is the

kind of feeder that Tina and Curtis are using. Ms Gourley states that some people had no problem getting bluebirds started as early as August by using it, if they are from a newly fledged group. Somtime the Dews found that it required a bit of enticement to attract the birds. If raisins, bits of dried fruit or apples are stuck on a piece of thorn bush twig or rose bush stem which is placed half in and half out of one of the entrance holes of the feeder, the bluebirds will spot the food and after eating it off the outside part of the thorn twigs, will find additional food inside the feeder by entering the hole opposite. Once the bluebirds have discovered the feeder and start eating, they will return during all seasons, the Dews have found. Tina cautions that when the young bluebirds find their way into a feeder, they sometimes cannot find their way out. The owner must be alert to let them out by lifting the hinged top. Adults have no trouble, but the young birds may perish if left in the box for too long a time, unable to get out.

How to Build
Your Own Bluebird House

The plan described in this section was developed by the Jackson (MS) Bluebird Project, under the sponsorship of the Jackson Audubon Society, which has been providing bluebird houses at cost to Mississippians over the past few years. The project now has over 30,000 bluebird houses in operation in Mississippi. There is hardly a town, village, or hamlet across the state that does not have at least ten or more houses in its midst. Reports received certainly show that there is really a difference being made in the bluebird population throughout the state. Annual Christmas bird counts attest to this fact also.

The Jackson Bluebird Project plan is easily made from boards that are ten inches wide and one-half inch thick. The sides and bottom are made from a four inch width and the top, back, and front are made from a five inch width. When ripping a ten inch wide board, you can get two four inch widths and a two inch strip to nail across the back for mounting the house. By laying out your pattern first you can get the total house from the least amount of lumber. Eight foot lengths may prove to be the most economical to purchase.

We suggest that you use aluminum nails or four penny cement coated nails which are one and one-fourth inches long, and that you use a one-fourth inch long, smooth shafted, galvanized roofing nail for the latch.

By following the assembly of the house in numerical order, as shown in the following plan, you will find that building the house is easy.

This recommended bluebird box conforms to the size and shape suggested by the North American Bluebird Society (NABS), and is best suited for the

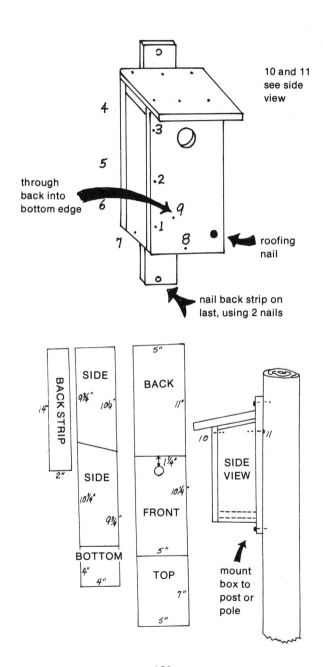

10 and 11
see side
view

4

.3

5

through
back into
bottom edge

6

.2

.9

.1

7

.8

roofing
nail

nail back strip on
last, using 2 nails

BACK STRIP

14"

2"

SIDE

9¾"

10¼"

SIDE

10¼"

9¾"

BOTTOM

4"

4"

5"

BACK

11"

1¼"

10¼"

FRONT

5"

TOP

7"

5"

SIDE
VIEW

10

11

mount
box to
post or
pole

Eastern and Western Bluebirds. Boxes for the Mountain Bluebird should conform to the same general size and shape but perhaps be of slightly larger dimensions. Bluebird houses are best made from cypress, a lasting wood that never needs painting and weathers to a beautiful grey color when left unpainted; exterior grade one-half or one-fourth inch thick plywood, western cedar, or white pine.

Cypress lumber is used extensively across numerous states for wooden fences, usually in six or eight foot lengths. By locating fence builders in the 'yellow pages' of the telephone directory, and then making inquiry, you can often find that they have a scrap pile of odds and ends from cutting fencing of varied lengths and widths. Usually these scraps are sold as kindling and you can pick up lengths sufficient to make your bird houses - in limited quantities. Also, there may be a hardwood mill in your vicinity that cuts cypress boards. If so, you can purchase resawed one inch thick cypress boards in six, eight, and ten foot lengths. Usually, however it is necessary to place your order in advance and agree to take a five hundred board foot minimum. This is for project making, of course, and is not the place to contact for a small amount of lumber for just a few bluebird houses.

Yard and garden stores and retail hardware stores usually stock a variety of bird houses. When purchasing a bluebird house, be sure that it conforms to the basic dimensions recommended for the bluebird and that it is made of wood that will properly withstand the weather elements.

The entrance hole of the bluebird house should be one and one-half inches in diameter, found to be sufficiently large to accomodate the Eastern and Western Bluebird, while the entrance hole for the Mountain Bluebird should be approximately one and five-eighths inches in diameter. We must state here, though, that we have witnessed many Mountain Bluebirds entering and leaving their houses in Estes Park, Colorado, which had the one and one-half inch diameter entrance holes. Bluebirds seemingly were having no trouble entering and leaving the houses. The debate on an exact size entrance hole for the Mountain Bluebird is still going on. The one and one-half inch diameter size will keep out the starling, one of the bluebird enemies.

No perch should be placed under the entrance hole. This omission is intentional to keep the House Sparrow from perching there and defying the bluebird, or any other bird, of its attempts to use the box. It is not wise to start out by giving a bluebird competitor that advantage. Bluebirds have no trouble holding on to the wood front without a perch. The large-headed, round, galvanized roofing nail on the front of the box (see plan) serves as a latch to hold the door closed and can easily be removed by inserting a knife blade, or screw driver end under the head of the nail to get it started. Then it can easily be removed with the fingers. When this is done, the side of the box can be opened for monitoring or cleaning out the house. A hole should be drilled for the roofing nail, using a drill bit that is just slightly larger than the diameter of the nail shaft, (usually a 9/64 inch) so that it will remove easily. After the nail is temporarily removed, the side door of the box will lift up, with the two nails at the top serving as hinges or pivot nails.

Some builders prefer a left side or front opening box. This same plan is easily modified for both. A top opening box, while readily accepted by bluebirds, may prove to be more difficult to look down into for monitoring.

Where to Locate the Bluebird House

Bluebird houses should be erected at a height of three to five feet above the ground in a reasonably open area, since the bluebirds will not nest in the woods and rarely in deep shade. Best is a totally open area or one with scattered trees and where the ground is kept free from underbrush and tall grasses. An added protection for young bluebird fledglings is the location of the box from twenty-five to fifty feet from a tree, so that their first flight from the box will permit them to fly to a tree and not land on the ground, where lurking predators may readily be. This nearby tree is not essential, however, and more often will not be found.

Bluebirds, too, will not usually nest closer together than 300 feet. However, to attract the first pair, houses may be placed closer together and then moved further apart from the first nesting pair. Always remember that there are exceptions to every rule.

Avoid facing the house toward the west, if possible, because of the hot afternoon summer sun. Also, if erecting the houses on fence posts that border a pasture (which usually is a desirable location), face the houses away from the cattle if possible, since the cattle often rub against the boxes and knock them down from their moorings, horses more so than cows.

In the southern states, boxes should be put up by the first of February, because the bluebirds begin to investigate nesting sites in February. A month later would serve for the northern states and still a month later than that for the Canadian provinces. Houses can be left up all winter to serve as roosting boxes during the cold winter days and nights for both bluebirds and other birds. Boxes should be cleaned out and repaired, if need be, by February first, however, for nesting readiness.

How to Mount a Bluebird House

After you have constructed your own bluebird houses, or purchased them, you are now ready to mount them properly. This should pose no problem (particularly if the boxes have mounting strips attached to the back), as is recommended in the plans already shown.

By using the two holes in the top and bottom

extension strips across the back of the box, it can be nailed, attached with screws, or wired to the existing post or pole. Sometimes the houses can be mounted on the side of a tree, provided the tree is on an edge of the scattered tree area, and not on the edge of a dense woods.

For those bluebird enthusiasts who may not have fence posts on which to mount bluebird houses, we have a recommendation to make that is both simple and inexpensive. Purchase from your hardware store or electrical supplier a ten-foot length of three-fourth inch diameter electrical conduit pipe. Then, using a hack saw, cut the ten-foot length into two five-foot lengths - thus making two poles. Purchase another ten-foot length of one-half inch diameter conduit and cut into two equal lengths. Then, after determining where you wish to locate your bluebird house, drive the one-half inch piece half into the ground, leaving about half of it above the ground. Care should be taken in driving the piece so as not to flatten the end left above the ground, hold a piece of wooden block across the pipe while driving it, to protect the pipe edge. Then mount your house to the five-foot length of three-fourth inch diameter size by using three fourth inch pipe brackets (also found at the hardware store). After the house is mounted near one end of the five-foot piece, slip the other end of the mounted piece of pipe over the protruding piece of pipe that you have driven into the ground. Using a hammer, drive the house mounted piece slightly into the ground to prevent its turning in the wind. Then grease the pole near the bottom

over about a one foot section to prevent fire ants
reaching the house.

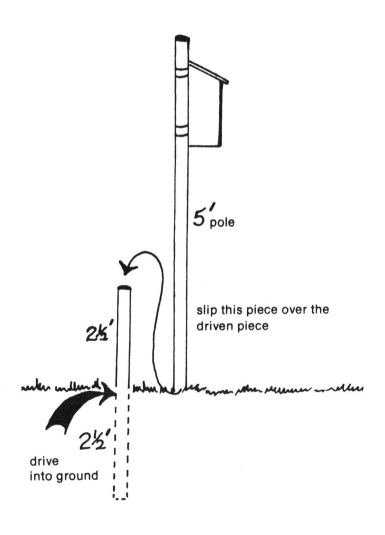

5' pole

slip this piece over the
driven piece

2½'

2½'

drive
into ground

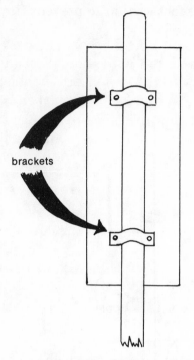

brackets

enlarged view showing house attached
with pipe brackets

Monitoring Your Bluebird House

Though it is not essential, we recommend that
you monitor your house/s regularly, preferably
every week during the nesting season. If you have
more than one house, then you are beginning a
"bluebird trail". The bluebird trail can contain as
many houses as you desire to erect. The longest

one is in Canada. It contains more than 7000 boxes and stretches across the provinces of Saskatchewan and Minetoba.

Of course, you and I must be more modest with our trails, for sure; but having more than one box adds appreciably to the enjoyment of bluebirds and gives added assistance to your efforts in helping to bring back the bluebirds to our areas. A bluebird trail can run in any direction and may go from one farm to another, in which case you have two trails.

Monitoring your boxes is the only way that you can keep up with what is going on inside them. We suggest, too, that you number your boxes. Use a wide tip, permanent ink, felt tip marker for this. It is much easier to use than paint and will last two or three years, easily remarked. Also chart your findings each time you monitor the boxes. By slowly approaching the box and quietly opening the door the parent bird(s) will not be frightened away permanently. This is the place, we have found, that you can talk to your birds without other human beings being unduly concerned. Conversation while approaching the bluebird house will give the adult birds that may be in the box an additional warning that you are approaching. Caution should be taken to avoid opening the boxes after the thirteenth day after the eggs are hatched so as not to cause the young birds to fledge prematurely. There is a mistaken belief that touching the nest of the young birds with your hand will cause the parents to desert the young and the nest. Often is is necessary to remove the old nest and even to remove a currently used nest if it is fouled with ants or blow fly larvae. When this occurs, a completely new nest should be made, as best you can from local grasses, and the young birds placed in the new nest that you have put into the bird house.

How to Maintain a Bluebird House

Bluebird boxes should be inspected in the month of February to make them ready for a new season. They may have been used during the winter months as roosting boxes, which is evidence that they need to be cleaned out befor nesting time. Inspect, clean, repair, and dust the boxes with 1% rotenone, Sevin dust, sulphur dust, or use a pyrethrin spray if there is mite infestation present. If there is evidence of opossum or raccoon tampering, make a predator guard (shown later in the narrative) and place it over the entrance hole of the box.

If, for some legitimate reason, it is necessary for you to open a bluebird house during the period when the young birds are between fifteen and twenty days of age a nest box reducer should be placed over the entrance hole. You should have some of these on hand always while monitoring bluebird houses. These are easily made from one-fourth inch thick exterior grade plywood or from masonite, or tempered wall board. Cut each one two inches square. Then drill a one inch hole through the center and small holes in each corner to accommodate a wood screw about one-half inch in length. The completed device is attached over the one and one-half inch diameter entrance hole, reducing it to one inch in diameter, just before it is necessary to open the box during the critical period. It is recommended that the four mounting holes be drilled into the houses in the spring before the nesting season begins, so that the reducers can easily be attached when needed by using only a screw driver and screws. Two screws placed in diagonally opposite holes is sufficient to hold the hole reducers in place. This simplifies the attachment process appreciably. CAUTION: Hole reducers should be removed as soon as fledging has been completed, or as soon as you have completed your box opening necessities. While the reducer is on the box the parent birds will continue to feed the nestlings through the reduced hole. The young birds cannot get out while the reducer is on the box. It is well to monitor closely the boxes with hole reducers during this period. Be sure that both adult birds have left the box before you attach the reducer for its would be a calamity indeed, if an adult bird were kept inside the box with the fledglings.

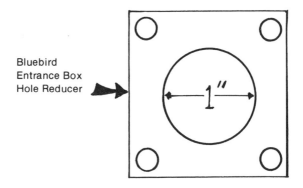

Bluebird
Entrance Box
Hole Reducer

How to Provide Bathing and Drinking
Facilities for the Bluebirds

A bird bath in the yard is an added attraction for bluebirds, particularly when bluebirds are nesting near your house. The location of the bird bath can make a difference in the degree of usage by the bluebirds and other birds. Certainly you must locate it in a place that is easily observed by you, so you won't miss the fun of watching the birds bathing and drinking. A location that is partially shaded and has a nearby limb, vine, or bush for the birds to light upon will enhance usage of the bird bath.

There are several types of bird baths on the market. The one most often seen is the concrete pedestal type with a large concrete basin. It is usually selected for its architectural beauty and not for its usefulness, for it is more difficult to maintain than the other types. A preferred type is one that has a removable basin of shallow depth and light weight, with a base that is easily moved about the yard when needed. We use a bird bath that has an aluminum basin, two inch, sloping depth, with a non-slip bottom. It fits on a triangular base of light weight metal. The basin is easily removed for washing at the yard hydrant and then replaced on its triangular base to be filled with fresh water daily.

Bird baths must be washed out daily and refilled with water. Only then will your birds use it to the fullest extent. It is well to remember that a non-tended bird bath is worse than no bath at all.

Winter usage of bird baths will continue, provided you are keeping the basin clean. You will need an electric heater to place in the water to keep the water from freezing. There are several types of heaters on the market, all of which seem to do the job. Just use an exterior extension cord and run it from the nearest electrical outlet, leaving it there during the winter season. The heater activates only when the water temperature is below forty degrees Fahrenhite, and deactivates when the water temperature reaches about fifty degrees. But you must keep water in the basin for it to work properly. Also, it will burn out quickly if left in a basin with no water.

Winter bathing by birds is continued, not as regularly as summer bathing, but you will be surprised to see birds bathing in very cold weather, and certainly they need a place to get their drinking water, when the ground water, ponds and lakes are frozen. The bird bath will also be used for drinking during dry weeks of all seasons.

How to Build a Bluebird Roosting Box

Bluebird landlords have found that bluebirds and other small birds, such as chickadees, titmice and nuthatches, will cluster together inside of a roosting box during the winter season. Especially is this true in very inclement weather. It is often found that a dozen or more birds will use a roosting box together.

Roosting boxes can vary in size from the regular bluebird box (which, too, serves as a roosting box if left up through the winter season) to a much larger size, about twelve inches by twelve inches in floor space and eighteen to twenty-four inches in height.

If you maintain a bluebird trail, you perhaps will desire to place several roosting boxes at intervals down the trail; or, if you are not a 'trail blazer', then one placed in your yard should prove to be a success.

Roosting boxes can be mounted on fence posts, tree trunks, or metal and wood poles. The boxes should not be placed too high above the ground, for bluebirds are accustomed to nesting at heights of three to five feet. However, bluebirds will accept roosting boxes that are mounted at greater heights.

The metal pipe or post has advantages over a tree trunk mount because it permits the addition of a conical or square metal guard, described later. A tree trunk or post mount can have added protection from predators, if they pose a problem in your area, by placing a predator guard over the entrance hole of the house.

In the following diagram will be found a typical nesting box. It can be mounted on any of the locations previously mentioned. This is the one time that we feel like recommending a bottom opening box, for the waste from the roosting birds accumulates on the box bottom, and by hinging the bottom at the back side it can easily be lowered for cleaning.

Since the roosting box serves as a roosting place out of the cold, no ventilation holes should be provided and only a very limited number of drain holes drilled through the floor (about four should

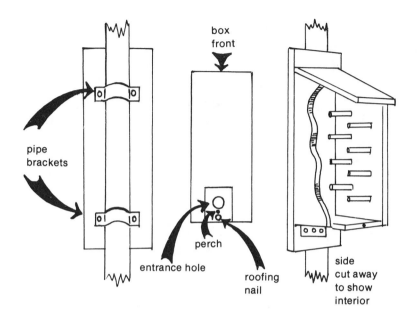

box
front

pipe
brackets

perch

entrance hole

roofing
nail

side
cut away
to show
interior

be sufficient), and of one-fourth inch diameter. Also, since heat rises, the entrance hole (only one) should be placed near the center bottom of the box front (see diagram). Here, too, we suggest that the roofing nail be used to lock the bottom in when the box is closed.

The roosting box entrance hole, as well as the hole in the predator guard, should be one and one-half inches in diameter. A larger hole will permit larger birds such as the starlings to enter the house - and the squirrel, too. Should the squirrel select the roosting box, it will proceed to enlarge the entrance hole and take the house over. We had this to happen to one of our roosting boxes. Not only did the little rascal enlarge the entrance hole but he also pulled out all of the roosting pins and left them on the floor of the house so he could build his bed of twigs and leaves on top of them. This can be prevented by placing a piece of sheet metal about four inches square over the hole through which you have drilled a one and one-half inch diameter hole through the center. If you have predator problems with raccoons, opossums, etc., add the wooden predator guard on top of the piece of sheet metal, as shown in the diagram.

The diagram shows a roosting box mounted to a metal post, using pipe brackets to hold the box to the pole. If you are planning to mount your box to a wood post or tree, then drill small holes above and below the house through which nails may be driven.

The roosting pins should be placed at intervals inside the house and they should be staggered as shown to add to the cleanliness from bird droppings. Also, pins on the opposite wall should be staggered as well. These pins can be made of one-fourth or one-half inch diameter dowel rods, purchased at your local hardware store. These should be cut about three inches in length, depending upon the size of your roosting box.

The roosting box should have a perch just below the entrance hole, since there is limited bird grasping space below the hole. This will give assistance to the bluebirds as they enter the hole.

PROTECTING YOUR BLUEBIRDS

The Threat of Other Small Birds

When monitoring your boxes, you may find that another bird than the bluebird has begun to use the box.

There are other birds that occasionally will build in your bluebird boxes, especially if they are placed near the woods. Among these other birds are the Tufted Titmouse, the Carolina Wren, the chickadee, the nuthatch, the Tree Swallow, and the House Sparrow. The Prothonotary Warbler may use the house, too, if it is near water.

There are individual characteristics that will help you determine what species of bird is using the box, if a complete, or almost complete nest is found. The wren uses a mass of leaves, twigs, rootlets, weed stalks, strips of bark, and debris. The wren nest is lined with feathers, hair, moss, wool, and fine grasses. The nuthatch nest is

145

similar to the wren's nest but has fewer twigs. The Tree Swallow and Violet Green Swallow nest primarily in Canada, the western and mountain states, and New England. They build their nest of straw, dry grasses, and bits of string, and line the nest with feathers and horsehair, if available. The bluebird nest is loosely built of fine grasses on top of coarser grasses and weed stalks. Sometimes, in the southern states especially, the bluebirds use pine straw alone for their nests. The House Sparrow nest is made of grasses and weeds and lined with feathers, some hair, string, plastic materials and most any other kind of debris that can be found. The nest is usually very compact and fills the bluebird house completely.

If there are eggs in the nest, you can determine the bird that is using the nest by the color and size of the eggs. The chickadee eggs are five to eight in number, oval to short oval shaped, smooth shell, very thin, with little or no gloss. They are small in size, about the size of a large English pea. They are white, rather evenly spotted and dotted with reddish brown, concentrated at the larger end.

The wren eggs are four to eight in number, oval to short-oval shaped, smooth shell with little or no gloss, white to pale pink, marked with brown spots, often concentrated at the larger end. They are about three-fourths of an inch in length. The nuthatch eggs are five to ten in number, oval to short-oval shaped, smooth shell, very little gloss, heavily marked with light brown to reddish brown spots, densest at the larger end, and about one-half inch in length. The swallow eggs are four to six in number, oval to long-oval shaped, smooth shelled, little or no gloss, and pure white, and are about five-eights of an inch in length.

The Prothonotary Warbler eggs are three to eight in number, oval to short-oval shaped, somewhat glossy, boldly and liberally spotted with brown shades over the entire egg. The eggs are about one-half inch in length.

The House Sparrow eggs are three to seven in number, five common, oval to short-oval shaped, smooth shell, slight gloss, white to greenish white, dotted and spotted with grays and browns. They are about three-fourths of an inch in length.

The bluebird eggs range from pure white to bluish white to deep blue, four to seven in number, five common, oval to short-oval shaped, smooth shell, glossy, and are unmarked. They are about three-fourths of an inch in length, with the Mountain Bluebird's eggs being slightly larger than the Eastern Bluebird's and Western Bluebird's eggs.

When one finds another bird's nest than a bluebird's, he may wonder what to do about it. Federal law prohibits the molestation of any bird's nest (especially if eggs are found) other than the House Sparrow nest, of the birds that are likely to be found nesting in the boxes. Destruction of both nest and eggs is recommended for the House Sparrow. Others should be left alone until fledging has been completed. Then nest removal is permitted.

The Threat of the House Sparrow

One of the reasons for the decline of the bluebird population can be attributed to the increase of the House Sparrow population. This House Sparrow is a prime usurper of bluebird nesting sites. When the House Sparrow decides to take over a bluebird house, it usually succeeds - for it is persistent to the "bitter end". The bluebird landlord must then come to the rescue of the bluebird.

A daily removal of the sparrow nest may be necessary, for in a week's time a complete nest with eggs will be found if left alone. Sometimes the sparrow will give up after one or two nest removals and move elsewhere, but if its has selected that particular site for its nesting, then discouragement is very difficult. Both sparrow nests and eggs, or young, should be destroyed in every case that they are found. Do not leave the removed nest nearby on the ground, for the little persistent bird will use from it to build another nest, almost while you are present. The House Sparrow is very agressive in appropriating the nest cavities of other birds. When it wants a bluebird house that is occupied by a bluebird family, it will go inside, fight off the adult bluebirds, and kill the young bluebirds and eject them from the house. Sometimes the sparrow is so persistent that trapping is the only way to eliminate him, particularly the male of the species, since it is the dominant of the pair.

How to Build a Huber Sparrow Trap

When trapping is necessary, one can use the Huber Sparrow Trap, *SIALIA* 3(1):95-95. The following illustration shows the Huber trap when it is set (Figure one) and when it is tripped (Figure two), *SIALIA* 4(1): 20.

Figure 1.

Interior view of the Huber Sparrow Trap. Figure 1 shows the trap when it is set.

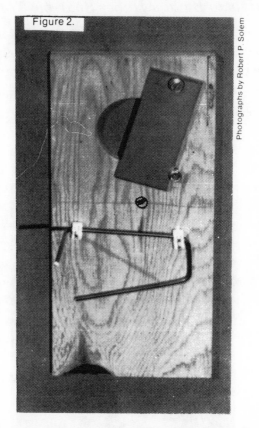

Photographs by Robert P. Solem

Figure 2.

Interior view of the Huber Sparrow Trap. Figure 2 shows the trap when it has been tripped. The entrance hole is now too small to allow the bird to leave the box.

When using the Huber trap, it is necessary for its user to be on hand to monitor the trap, for the trap will catch any bird that enters the house, and survival inside on a very hot day may be for only a short duration - thus, making it necessary to be on hand to let out desirable birds that may be caught. The trap should be removed when the trapping period is over.

We have added a further adaptation of our own to the Huber trap, to make it suitable for left, right, and front opening boxes, since the presentations are for a clip-on in a top opening box. You will notice that by making a single addition of a small screw through the center of the trap board, it can be secured to the inside of the bird box front by using a short, stubby screw driver and inserting your hand into the box to screw the trap to the front inside. This type of screw driver can usually be found at the hardware store, or you can modify one of your own that has a plastic handle with a short metal end by cutting off the handle to the desired length, which is about three inches total length. A bolt and nut may be used instead of the screw to attach the trap.

Requirements for a Huber trap

A-3" x 8½" plywood
B-1¾" entrance hole
C-Steel plate (⅛" x 1¼" x 3")
D-Brass rod (3/32" diameter) for trigger
E-Insulated electrical staples for hinges
F-Stop screw #6 x ½" round-head wood screw)
G-Pivot screw (#6 x ½" round-head wood screw)
H-U-shaped clip

How to build the Huber trap

- Cut a piece of plywood (A) approximately 3" x 8" (or to a size that fits your nestbox).

- Before drilling the 1¾" entrance hole (B), be sure that it will align with the hole in your nestbox.

- Cut a steel plate (C). Drill ⅛" hole in the steel plate for the pivot screw. (Thin plywood or sheet metal may be substituted.)

- Bend a 10½" brass rod (3/32" diameter) to the shape shown in Figure 1. Bend the lower part of the rod forward 90⁰, as shown in Figure 2. This is the trigger (D). (A heavy guage coat hanger may be cut for this.) File the ends smooth.

- Install the trigger (D) on the plywood with two insulated electrical staples (E) that will serve as hinges.

- Install the steel plate (C) with the pivot screw (G). The dotted lines show the steel plate in the closed position (C), after the trigger has been tripped.

- Bend a brass rod or coat hanger wire into a U-shaped clip (H) and use this to wedge the plywood trap against the inside of the nestbox.

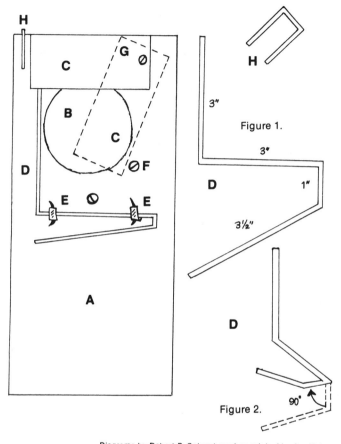

H

C

G ⦰

B

C

D

⦰ F

E ◐ E

A

3″

Figure 1.

3″

D

1″

3½″

D

90°

Figure 2.

Diagrams by Robert P. Solem based on original by Joe Huber.

When the sparrow has been caught in the Huber trap, it then becomes necessary to remove the sparrow from the trap. Do not open the door of the trap to remove the sparrow, for it will manage to slip out before you can catch it. A better way is to take a plastic garment bag, from the dry cleaners, and secure the top end with a rubber band, piece of tied string, or a "twist-em" from bread loaf, or otherwise. Then, slip the bag down over the house and post. Now remove the roofing nail latch but do not open the door. Secure the bottom of the bag by tying a string around the bag and post. Next, open the door of the house by holding your hand against the outside of the house and opening the door from outside the bag. The sparrow will fly into the bag, to be removed as you see fit. If you are reluctant to destroy the sparrow, and prefer to carry it to a distant place instead, be sure that you carry it at least five miles from your bird house or it will return again.

How to Use a Sparrow Trapping Cage

Another type of sparrow trap that has been found to be very successful is the trapping cage. This type, when baited with bird feed, bread crumbs, doughnuts, or other scraps, will attract the House Sparrow and contain him for removal and relocating or destroying. After sparrows are trapped, they enter a center holding compartment so that the trap can be reset to catch others. Resetting is easily done by simply raising the two springed doors until they click into the triggers. Action is gentle and will not harm the birds. Of course, the trap cannot distinguish among bird species and will catch any bird that enters and triggers the door closed. So, one must be alert to monitor every little while to let out birds that are not House Sparrows. The trap is made of heavy gauge galvanized wire and has two trap compartments, one on each end. The trap can be placed on the ground or easily attached to a fence or post for removal when desired. It comes fully assembled and can be purchased from some of the birding supply catalogues listed elsewhere in this book.

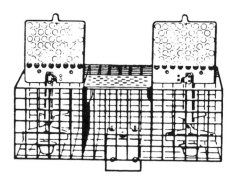

Sparrow Trapping Cage

Latest Idea to Repel the House Sparrow

So states Mary Janetatos, Executive Director of the North American Bluebird Society (Mailed out insert flyer, NABS). She comments further:

> The device shown in this drawing is the latest thing I've heard of to discourage sparrows. A young woman in Gaithersburg, Maryland found that the bluebirds were undaunted by an air-sock (wind sock) which trailed on top of the bluebird box. She told me about it and I immediately revised it as you see in the drawing. The sparrows

155

have not entered the nesting box since putting this up, but the bluebirds come every day, and even perch on top of the little flag pole. Please try it and report the results to the North American Bluebird Society - and get others to try it. The major drawback, as I see it, would be the attractiveness to a two-legged vandal, if it were used on public roads. Anyway, the whole idea works as a scarecrow does. It's just the ticket for those who hate "doing in" the sparrows.

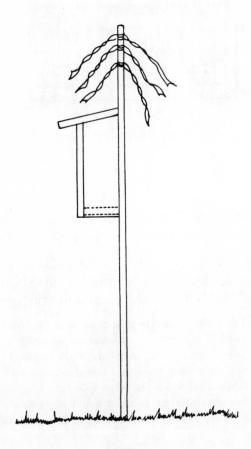

The Threat of Predators

Sometimes the bluebird landlord finds evidence of predators on his bluebird trail or in his bluebird house. The most likely predators are: squirrels, raccoons, opossums, house cats, porcupines (northern states and Canada), and sometimes snakes, usually non-poisonous type.

How to Prevent Entrance Hole Enlargements

One preventive measure to use in preventing entrance hole enlargement on bluebird houses is to use a stapling gun and drive one-fourth inch staples into the wood around the entrance hole edge when the house is erected or is being cleaned out. This will keep the woodpeckers and the squirrels from enlarging the hole, and also it is easily accomplished. Tacks can be driven into the wood around the hole in a similar fashion, if desired. This will accomplish the same result.

Another procedure is to cut a one and one-half inch hole through a piece of tin or aluminum metal that is about two and one-half to three inches square and secure it over the entrance hole with small nails or tacks. Holes for the tacks or nails can be made before attaching by using a small drill bit or driving a somewhat larger nail through the metal piece before attaching. This kind of attachment can also be made over an enlarged hole to reduce it to the proper size. CAUTION: If the metal piece is so large that the surface below the entrance hole is covered beyond about one and one-half inches, a small piece of sand paper, or emery paper, or similar rough surface, should be stapled across the metal below the hole to provide the birds gripping ease that may not be sufficient from the metal plate. Still another device that can be used successfully is a large metal washer with a one and one-half inch diameter center hole. This can be attached over the entrance hole by using carpet tacks to hold the washer over the entrance hole. This size of washer is not always readily available at all hardware stores. A machine shop should be able to supply it.

How to Add Predator Guards
to a Bluebird House

An economical type of predator guard to prevent molestation by the opposum, raccoon, and house cat in areas where these predators have given trouble, is the use of a simple block of wood added to the thickness of the house entrance hole area. Out of a block of wood about six inches long from a piece of "two-by-four" lumber (usually a nearby construction project will have small pieces in their scrap pile), drill a one and one-half inch diameter hole in the block of wood so that it can be mounted over the existing bluebird entrance hole. Attach the block to the house by using wood screws through four holes bored through the corners of the block (see diagram). Select screws that will easily go through the holes that you have made, and about one-fourth inch longer than the thickness of the block, so that the block can be attached to the house.

Since the predator blocks are so easily made, we suggest that you have several available to use when needed. Some prefer to attach these to all of their houses in the spring when they are making the houses ready for the new season. The guards seemingly make little or no difference to the bluebirds in their usage of the house. The Dews have these on all their houses.

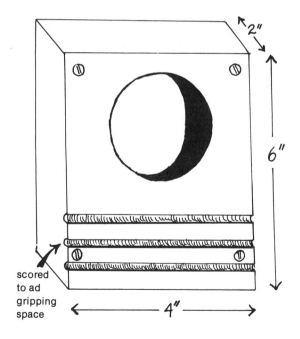

scored
to ad
gripping
space

This added thickness of the house front will prevent these mentioned predators from bending their elbows when reaching into the houses. The predator is unable then to reach its paw down into the box sufficiently to reach the baby birds. Also, increasing the bluebird house depth when building it, so that it has a twelve or fourteen inch depth, will keep the nest and its contents out of the reach of the inquisitive visitors. Do not be concerned about the ability of the young bluebirds to climb up the interior front wall of the house to reach the entrance hole. They can easily climb any wooden box surface.

How to Build a Conical Predator Guard

Predators such as opossums, raccoons, snakes, house cats, and the like can be prevented from reaching your bluebird house by using a conical predator guard. This is easily made from a sheet of galvanized metal or aluminum and in the following will be found a cutting pattern for this.

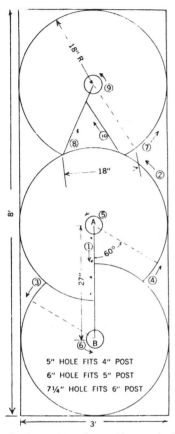

18" R

18"

8'

5" HOLE FITS 4" POST
6" HOLE FITS 5" POST
7¼" HOLE FITS 6" POST

60°

27"

A

B

3'

Cutting pattern for making conical
predator guards from sheet metal.
Numbered arrows indicate cutting
sequence and direction. (Courtesy
U.S. Fish and Wildlife Service)

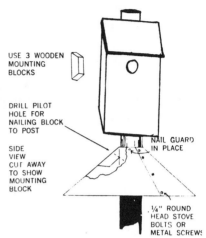

USE 3 WOODEN
MOUNTING
BLOCKS

DRILL PILOT
HOLE FOR
NAILING BLOCK
TO POST

SIDE
VIEW
CUT AWAY
TO SHOW
MOUNTING
BLOCK

NAIL GUARD
IN PLACE

¼" ROUND
HEAD STOVE
BOLTS OR
METAL SCREWS

Assembly and mounting details for
conical predator guard.

Sheet metal or aluminum often can be purchased from the local hardware store in half
sheets, which will be sufficient. If not from the

hardware store, then the sheet metal store will provide this. For your conical guard we recommend that nothing less than a thirty-six inch diameter piece of sheet metal be used. Follow these simple directions to make the guard. First, scribe a thirty-six inch circle on your metal sheet. Next, draw a radius from the outer edge to the center point. Then, using tin snips, cut down the radius line from the circle edge to the center point. Draw a circle for your center cutout for the pole to go through. A five-inch diameter hole will fit a four-inch post, a six-inch diameter hole will fit a five-inch post and a seven and one-fourth inch diameter hole will fit a six-inch diameter post.

Now, mark off a sixty degree angle wedge from the radius edge in either direction. Then, drill three or four small holes through the circular sheet as shown in the middle circle. Pull the split sheet together so that the edges overlap. Drill holes through the under layer, using the already drilled holes as a pattern. The two pieces will then be conical shaped, ready to place around the pole. We recommend using split rivets, one-fourth inches long, to brad the sheets together around the fence post. You may drill small holes around the upper edge of the center hole to nail the guard in place on the post. Additional reinforcement can be made by cutting a wooden wedge as shown and used for attaching the conical sheet to the post. If you choose not to do this yourself, seek out a carpenter for help.

How to Build a Square Predator Guard

Curtis Dew has developed and uses his own guard for the Dews' bluebird houses and claims them to be entirely satisfactory. The secret of their success is size and placement, They should be placed as close to the bottom of the bluebird house as possible. This prohibits the predator from seeing the house from below.

Materials used:
- -1 piece of aluminum or galvanized metal, three feet square
- -2 pieces of one inch by three inch strips from the same metal
- - pop rivets or split rivets, or nuts and bolts
- - tin snips
- - hammer
- - Drill and bit (size of bit depends upon the size of the rivets of nuts and bolts that you plan to use)

Find the center of the sheet by drawing two diagonals across the sheet. Then, starting at one corner, cut to the center with the tin snips. Next cut out the center to the diagram. Make it the size of your mounting post or pole. Wrap the guard around the post or pole and pull the edges together and lap one over the other enough for you to install rivets or bolts and nuts. Fold the corners of the sheet under for safety. Fasten the guard to the post or pole with the pieces of one by three inch metal strips. A second alternative to cutting out the

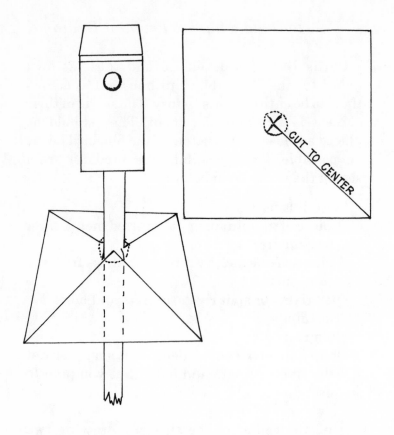

center of the guard for attachment is to cut the first diagonal from corner to center as shown in the diagram, leaving attachment ends at the center of the cut. If you use strips for attachment, a thicker metal is actually better for the strips as it gives more bracing for the guard in strong winds. Small corner braces, about three inches long, with holes already in them, are readily available at the hardware stores. These can be bent to meet the angle slope of the guard. If attaching to a wooden post or pole, roofing nails may be used to attach the strips or braces to the post. Still another technique would be to drive four nails through the top center edges of the metal guard. Wood screws may also be used to attach the guard.

The Threat of Insects

How to Combat the Fire Ant

A nest box infested with fire ants is a great disappointment to any bluebird trail monitor. Instead of finding healthy bluebirds, that he had watched develop, the bluebirder finds a deserted nest containing bare bird bones and feathers, the result of fire ant infestation - which can happen suddenly.

The predatorial ant is said to have found its way by boat, first into Alabama, then other states, from South America about fifty years ago. Despite years of chemical warfare, the fire ant has spread from state to state across the south. It has now invaded untold acres of farms, forests, parks, and yards in most southern states and is gradually moving northward every year.

Even though you may not have experienced, as yet, fire ant calamity with your bluebirds, be aware that it can happen at any time. If there are fire ant hills in your area and particularly near your bluebird boxes, it is time to take some precautions.

In the search for a means of preventing fire ant infestation in bluebird boxes, we have looked for some way to keep these insects from reaching the bird house. Killing the ants is a losing cause in most cases, and we have come up with the following technique. By inserting wooden spools (of the type household thread is wound upon) over the box mounting nails before they are driven into the fence post, and then coating the spools with an adequate grease, a barrier is created (see figure). Fire ants will not cross the grease to get into the bird house. We have carried out experiments with captured ants to assure the efficacy of this technique. The results demonstrate that it works. Through testing we found that STP Oil Treatment was the most long lasting grease substance. Other substances, such as Vaseline, and automobile greases hardened in three to four weeks in the hottest summer days. Once the grease has hardened, the ants can walk across the barrier. So, it is important to keep the lubricant soft and active.

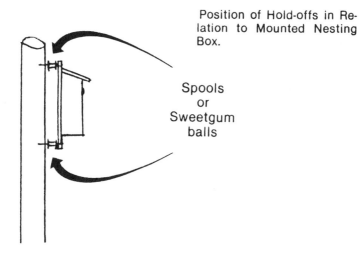

Position of Hold-offs in Relation to Mounted Nesting Box.

Spools
or
Sweetgum
balls

As an alternative to using wooden spools, which are becoming harder to get, since thread is now often being wound on plastic spools, the dried ball of the Sweetgum tree may be substituted. It has several advantages. It is almost indestructible and will not split or crumble when a nail is driven through it, and is readily available in most areas. The projections should be broken off prior to nailing to create a round ball. The small holes where the "horns" break off even effer extra holding power for the grease.

Whether you use spools, sweetgum balls, or some object of your own devising, it is important to use a well greased hold-off to prevent fire ants from reaching your bluebird houses. Carry grease with you as you monitor your boxes. Touching up with a one-inch paint brush, or a spatula, is quick and easy.

One may raise the question, "Why not just paint a circle of oil or grease around the fence post to keep the ants from reaching the boxes?" The answer is that the fire ants will find another way to reach the box, like crawling down the barbed wire or wire strands, or the cross bars, or other devious methods of reaching their goal. They are shrewd insects. Even spreading fire ant poison around the base of the post, which is recommended as a deterrent, will not keep them from reaching their destination in another way.

How to Build Nest Elevators to Control Blow Fly Infestation

We have never had blow fly infestation in any of

our boxes. While blow flies are not widespread, it is disappointing, indeed, to find young birds infested with blow fly larvae. It may then be too late to do anything about the problem. Also, predetermining when this may occur is not possible. Therefore, a preventive measure is best pursued, particularly when it is so easily accomplished, as recommended by Ira L. Campbell in *SIALIA* 6 (2): 70. He has found that placing a small piece of hardware cloth in the bottom of the nesting box before nesting season begins will eliminate losses of young birds because of the blow fly. The bluebirds will build their nests on top of the wire.

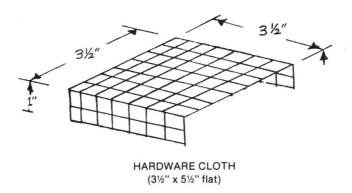

HARDWARE CLOTH
(3½" x 5½" flat)

Cut a piece of one-half inch mesh hardware cloth to a size of three and one-half inches by five and one-half inches when flat, and bend the two ends as shown in the diagram. The wire will then fit into the floor of the four by four inch interior of the box. The hardware cloth can be bought from almost any hardware store in small widths from a large roll. Purchase the smallest width available, for this will make several nesting elevators. Use tin snips to cut the hardware cloth and cut it just outside of the squares that you intend to use. In this way you will have a full square each time. By placing these platforms in your bluebird houses before nesting season begins, should the blowfly be encountered, the blowfly eggs and larva will fall through the nest and not remain in the nest to hatch.

How to Control the Wasps

While monitoring your bluebird house or boxes on your trail, you may find that a wasp nest has been started inside the box. Usually the nest is suspended from the ceiling of the box. When you open the door of the box, the wasps, usually two in number, will fly away immediately, particularly if it is a new nest. The nest then can be pinched out and destroyed. If the nest is larger and contains several wasps, they may resist being driven away. In such case, we suggest that you spray the nest and wasps with a pyrethrin spray. This will either drive them away or exterminate them. Then you can remove the nest.

There are a couple of preventive measures that can be taken to help discourage wasp building in your bluebird houses. One of these is to wipe some grease, like Vaseline, across the ceiling of the house and down each interior box side for a couple of inches, perhaps to the top of the entrance hole. This often discourages wasps building. Caution should be taken not to use the grease below the entrance hole, for then it may be rubbed off by the bluebirds entering and leaving the house, which is not good for the bluebirds or your efforts at wasp prevention. The other and safer method is to rub the ceiling and the interior sides with Ivory soap, which will discourage the wasps from building, and too, will not grease the adult birds should they come into contact with it.

After bluebirds have selected a house and have begun their nest building, the bluebirds will take care of any wasps that attempt to use the house.

QUESTIONS AND ANSWERS
ABOUT BLUEBIRDS

Q. When should I put up my bluebird houses?

A. Southern states - by February 1
Northern states - by March 1
Canada by - April 1

This does not mean that houses cannot be put up after these dates or before. These are the dates for receiving full season results. Remember that bluebirds will raise two, three and sometimes four or five broods a year. The latest nesting date that I have had is September, which is an exception, of course.

Q. Do I remove the nest after each fledging?

A. Yes, because the bluebirds will seldom use the same nest for a second brood. They usually will build another nest on top of the old nest, or leave

172

MOTHER BLUEBIRD INCUBATING
(SHE LIKED TO BE PHOTOGRAPHED)

PHOTO BY REBER LAYTON

the house for another site. So, if you remove the nest, you are providing a better nesting place. Too, you can dust the house interior with 1% rotenone powder, Sevin dust or sulphur dust, to keep down mite infestation. Also, if the nest is not removed and the bluebirds build another nest on top of the old one, the height of the new nest will be raised closer to the entrance hole, permitting predators to reach down into the house much more easily to destroy eggs, young, or adult birds.

Q. How often may I look into my bluebird house during the nesting season?

A. As often as is necessary; every day if need be. By using a quiet approach to the house so as not to unduly disturb the bluebirds, they will not mind your intrusion. Often I have had the mother bird stay on the nest while I opened the door to look inside, and even to photograph the bird (see photo). Particularly is this the case when the mother bird is incubating or laying eggs.

Q. Within recent weeks we have had a bluebird fly into our patio glass door with such force that it "knocked itself out". We placed the stunned little bird on the patio table top and watched it. Soon it revived and flew away. Is this a common trait and what can we do to eliminate this hazard?

A. First, it is not a rarity among birds. It is unusual among bluebirds, since it is seldom that one finds bluebirds flying into windows and doors, perhaps because bluebirds are still scarce among human habitats. Second, there is little one can do to prevent this occurrence. Not always are birds that fly into glass obstructions as fortunate as the one you mentioned, for many do not survive this calamity when it occurs. They often fly into the windows or doors with such force that they kill themselves in the act. The most plausible reason why birds fly into windows and doors is that birds are not always able to see the glass obstructions, thinking them to be an open passage into an area similar to the one behind them, caused by the reflection of the wooded area that they are leaving. Frequently birds take shortcuts across porches and patios, whether under roof or in the open. This occurrence is more likely to happen when people are feeding their feathered friends during the winter months and more birds are assembled near glass windows and doors. You did the best thing we know of, placing the stunned bird in a protected place until it recuperates. Be on the alert, however, for the lurking shrike bird, for it may just pounce upon the stunned one, particularly if it is a small bird, and fly off with it for a full meal. We had this happen to a little Pine Siskin that was recovering from a glazed encounter, much to our surprise while watching. We did not know the shrike was there. This occurence, we hasten to add, is a rarity.

Q. What should I do if I find a wasp nest inside the
   bluebird house?

A. The obvious answer is to remove the wasp nest.
   I have found that by monitoring houses weekly
   after nesting season begins, the wasp nest
   when just begun will only be small in size, with
   only a couple of wasps inhabitants. These two
   wasps will usually fly away immediately and
   you can remove the nest. However, if you wait
   another week, the wasp group will be larger and
   so will the nest, making it more difficult to
   combat them. Once the bluebirds have begun
   nesting in the box, however, they seem to take
   care of the wasps on their own. If you use a
   spray to eliminate the wasps, be sure that it is a
   pyrethrin spray, for many sprays on the market
   are harmful to birds.

Q. Will bluebirds nest inside of our cities?

A. Usually they will not. The bluebird prefers an
   open area, in an urban or rural setting. However, there are exceptions. They will build in
   communities on the edge of towns and cities,
   particularly where they had already begun
   nesting before many people houses were built.

Q. Will bluebirds build in houses that are close together?

A. The usual answer is no. Bluebirds are somewhat territorial. But, there again, we have exceptions to this rule. I prefer to inform my inquirers that it makes no difference how close together the houses are placed when attracting the first pair. The more houses, the more opportunities. Then, after the first pair begin their building, move the other houses further apart. About 300 feet apart is recommended, particularly for a bluebird trail. I recall going with a friend, at his request, to his farm to give advice about box location on his bluebird trail. When we began to observe the trail, I noticed that he had placed the houses on alternate fence posts, down a pasture fence row. There were six houses, about fifteen to twenty feet apart. Upon observing this, I casually suggested that perhaps, to start with, they might be too close together. We opened the door of the first house and there was a bluebird nest inside with four blue eggs. We went to the second house. It had a bluebird nest with two eggs inside. I was beginning to feel somewhat embarrassed by this time when, upon opening the door of the third house, there were young bluebirds inside. At this point I had to remark to my friend, "Just forget what I have said. This defies explanation". To bring this to a close, there were five bluebird nests in the six boxes. Unbelievable! So, there are exceptions to almost every rule, though usually not as great as this turned out to be.

Q. What can I do if I find a bluebird house with young bluebirds inside but covered with fire ants?

A. You would be lucky to get there before it was too late. Brush or wipe off the ants with a soft cloth and place the young birds in a container, if you have one handy, or otherwise, place them on the ground where there are no ants, until you have cleaned all the young birds. Then proceed to remove the nest from the house and remove all of the ants from the house and the fence post. Rid the post of ants by spraying with a pyrethrin spray. If you have none with you, then brush off all of the ants with a sprig of grass or limb. Then build a new grass nest for the young birds. No, you can't do as well as the mother bird could, but most any type of nest you build will be accepted by the parent birds, and the young birds cannot complain. Make a cup shape for the nest and then place the young birds inside. The parents will soon come back to the house and begin looking after their young. They would even thank you if they could. It's worth a try and usually it will work.

CAUTION: If you get stung by the fire ants, take immediately almost any allergy tablet or capsule. This will do wonders in eliminating the burn and itching. If you have too many stings, consult your physician as soon as possible. This is important! Keep gardening gloves in your kit for this. And Rhulispray for quick relief.

Q. Will bluebirds build in houses that are made of PVC pipe or in one gallon plastic milk containers?

A. Yes, they will. However, not as readily as in recommended wooden houses. If you do use the round PVC pipe, be sure to use pipe that has at least a six-inch diameter in order to provide sufficient room for the nest, and, very important, too, is to provide adequate ventilation holes for the houses, and drain holes to let out rain water that may collect inside. Gallon jugs have been found to be accepted by bluebirds, but they should be used as temporary measures, for they lack beauty and because of their thin walls they become very hot in the summer heat. Their transparency should be painted out to attract the bluebirds.

Q. Which is preferred, a side opening box or a top opening box?

A. The bluebirds don't seem to mind. It is a matter of choice to the bluebird landlord. Some prefer the top opening type because the birds are less likely to be disturbed when monitoring. We recommend the side opening type house because often the top opening ones are more difficult to look down into. We have not found the birds to be disturbed unduly when they are in a side opening house. For trail monitoring, the side opening type has distinct advantages. Do not use a bottom opening box, for it is almost impossible to monitor. There is a technique used by some that does not require opening the box at all for monitoring. That is, to carry a flashlight and mirror when on the trail and by focusing the mirror above the entrance hole and flashing the light into the mirror, one can observe the contents. This requires some practice before one becomes adept at it.

Q. What is the best time of year to select fences for bluebird house installation?

A. During the summer months or early fall months is best, while the vegetation is still alive. If selection is made during the winter months, often it is found later that tall grasses, vines, and shrubs grow up around the post which were not evident during the winter months, causing a disappointment to the bluebird landlord. Bluebirds prefer a clear area for their nesting site.

Q. Will bluebirds build in a bluebird house that is erected near a human dwelling?

A. Yes, in fact several bluebird landlords have reported that they had little luck in attracting bluebirds until they moved the bluebird house to a position about ten feet from the den window and next to the patio. Immediately the bluebirds built and raised their family next to the much-used patio. Bluebirds and humans usually are compatible.

Q. Will bluebirds eat at my feeders in the winter time?

A. Not at the usual feeders, but once they have begun to use a bluebird feeder, they will continue to use it during winter months. Your best blue-bird feeding opportunity is to provide a feeder of the type used by the Dews to feed raisins, berries and fruit. One bluebird landlord has told us of her gathering rose hips and freezing them for winter use, taking out a few daily from the freezer for bluebird feeding. You can also freeze other kinds of berries and fruits to give the bluebirds in the winter time. Remember that bluebirds do not feed on the usual winter bird feeder fares, and must be enticed to use any type of feeder. Even raisins must be cut in two pieces.

Q. Will bluebirds eat suet?

A. Not when fed in the usual suet feeder. However, when bluebirds have begun to use a bluebird feeder of the type the Dews have, then they will feed on suet also (in very small pieces), if it is placed inside the feeder along with the raisins.

Q. If a calamity should occur and the two adult bluebirds are both killed during the nesting time, with young bluebirds waiting to be fed inside their house, what can the bluebird landlord do?

A. Human feeding of young birds of any bird species is difficult. Your chances are best if the young birds are about to fledge. You may be able to feed them sufficiently until they fledge. Recommended food includes insects, such as: caterpillars, moths, crickets, meal worms (from a pet shop), canned dog food of a good grade, lean ground meat, hard-boiled egg yolk that includes well crushed egg shell, raw liver, raisins cut in half. Do not give water. The foods used will provide a sufficient amount of water until the orphans can get their own. Feeding should be about every twenty minutes, from dawn to dusk, and by the same person preferably. So, you can begin to see some of the problems in feeding. Place bites in mouth.

Better than feeding is to find another bluebird house with young bluebirds still being fed by their parents and place the orphans in the nest with the others. The parent birds usually will adopt them and feed them along with their own, even if there is an age difference. If you do not have an active house with bluebird young, and do not know where one is to be found, call your bluebird friends, or your local Audubon chapter, or Natural Science Museum to have them suggest available prospects. But, you will have to be quick about this, for bluebird young will soon perish if not fed.

Q. When I go out to monitor my trail of bluebird houses, what tools and materials should I have in my knapsack?

A. This is an excellent question. It is well to be prepared when going on the trail. Your bag should have these items: hammer, a few nails (four penny cement coated nails or aluminum nails to repair the house, one and one-fourth inch long galvanized roofing nails for the lock, six penny common nails to secure the house to its mount), a small roll of maleable iron wire (used to be called stove-pipe wire) if your houses are mounted on metal posts, a screw driver to pry where necessary, a pair of common slip-joint pliers, a can or bottle of grease, a wide tip felt permanent ink marker, 1% rotenone powder, Sevin dust, or sulphur dust, small roll of black plastic electrician's tape, a few hole reducers and predator guards, a bottle of drinking water and vial of antihistamine tablets in case of fire ant bites and a first aid kit in your car. Gloves.

Q. I would like to set up a bluebird trail but we have no rural land. How can I go about finding an appropriate fenced area to inquire about?

A. Your question is well put. Inquire about is the

proper approach. One should never erect his bluebird houses on someone's land without permission to do so. However, there is a first step that is needed before approaching a landlord for his permission, that is, the proper selection of a land site. We have already mentioned the selection when the undergrowth and weeds can be checked out. Once you have determined that the property you have selected for your bluebird houses will be kept free of undergrowth, then ask the land owner. We have been guilty of selecting sites during the winter months that were clear of grasses and vines, only to come back in summer after we had erected the houses, to find them covered with undergrowth, and not selected by any bluebirds.

Once you have found such a cleared site, there is usually little or no problem in procuring permission to erect houses and getting permission to monitor them during the nesting season. Often the landlord will assist you in the monitoring during the nesting season, and then you have made another bluebird lover.

Q. What is the best chemical spray to use in combating the gypsy moth so as not to be harmful to bluebirds and other wildlife?

A. The Rachel Carson Council, 8940 Jone Mill Road, Chevy Chase, Maryland, 20815 recommends the use of bacillus thuringiensis rather than chemical insecticides for the control of the gypsy moth (*SIALIA* 4[3]:82.) You should write to this authoratative council for complete information on this subject.

Q. Is there a law prohibiting the hand raising of birds?

A. Yes, there certainly is a law prohibiting this. Under dire circumstances, such as the sudden death of both parent birds with young that cannot be fed unless a human acts as foster parent, should one attempt to raise young birds. And, even then the birds should be released as quickly as possible. A better solution would be to find another bluebird pair, as we have previously stated, and give them the task of raising the orphans with their own. It is unlawful to hand raise any native bird without a federal permit. Permits, if given, are obtained from the nearest district office of the United States Fish and Wildlife Service, Law Enforcement Division, U.S. Department of the Interior. We wish to discourage attempts at procurement, since rarely can one justify sufficiently his being given a permit.

Q. I have often thought that I would like to band some of my young bluebirds for future identification. Is a permit necessary and how do I go about getting one?

A. A serious bird watcher may sometimes become interested in a more scientific study of birds. One possibility is then bird banding, that is trapping birds by specified harmless means and attaching to their legs tiny metal identification tags. This must not be done merely for amusement; indeed, there are legal restrictions on who can be a bird bander. There are certain qualifications which must be met. Control of banding is in the hands of the United States Fish and Wildlife Service, which alone issues permits for bird banding. To be accepted one must not only meet the qualifications of the Service, but be willing to accept their outlined responsibilities for such scientific work. Once he has qualified and is issued a permit, he will be equipped with thin aluminum bands to put around birds' legs for identification, such as "32-245689" or "A-569758" or "F and W Serv. Wash. D.C." These official bands and records are supplied to the bird bander free of charge by the government, but each one must be accurately accounted for.

Lately government policy regarding bird banding has become increasingly strict. A moratorium has been declared on the issuance of new bird banding permits. A definite need for ornithological information is required now for prospective banders, rather than merely to be "ready, willing, and able". New permits to qualified banders are issued as old permits are retired.

The Fish and Wildlife Service states that the "only justifiable purpose for placing a U.S. Fish and Wildlife Service band on a bird is to generate new scientific information which accrues from the banding and/or the subsequent recovery of that bird." The laboratory states: (1) that a person eligible for banding should be capable of, and prepared to submit legible, accurate, and complete records whenever requested, (2) that bandings must be for quality rather than quantity. Before placing a band on a bird, one should ask "Why am I banding this bird?" and whether the bird can be accurately aged and sexed. If not, then why band? Thus "banding with a purpose" is important.

Q. I live in the northwest, in Western Bluebird territory, and I am having difficulty keeping the swallows from taking over all of my bluebird houses. What can I do to prevent this?

A. The simplest answer is to place a second house in the immediate vicinity of the house that has been chosen by the swallows. Both bluebirds and swallows will live side by side and by using more boxes, perhaps you will solve your problem.

Q. Is there a certain elevation that Western Bluebirds prefer for their nesting sites?

A. Most of the Western Bluebirds are concentrated above the 600 foot level, which oldtimers refer to the "bluebird line". However, here again, there are exceptions to this rule.

Q. Is there a supplier of numbered aluminum tags where I may purchase numbers for my bluebird houses on my bluebird trail?

A. We know of one local source for these: Forestry Suppliers, Inc., 205 West Rankin Street, P.O. Box 8397, Jackson, MS 39204. There may be others also.

Q. Is there a Canadian group that is active in bluebirding that I may write?

A. Yes, there are many across Canada, for our Canadian friends have been quite active blue-birders for many years and are doing a great part in bringing back bluebirds to North America. Perhaps one of the most active groups is that headed by Bryan Shantz, biologist at the Ellis Bird Farm. His address is: P.O. Box 5501, Red Deer, Alta T4N 6N1, Canada. Bryan is a biologist and nature photographer who is employed by the Union Carbide Plant to monitor the nest box trail on the Ellis Bird Farm and at the Union Carbide Plant also. He oversees over 500 boxes.

Q. Where can I get a set of slides about bluebirds?

A. The North American Bluebird Society, Box 6295, Silver Spring, MD 20906-0295 has an excellent slide show that can be rented for $10.00

or purchased for $55.00. The set contains 141 collated cardboard-framed 35mm slides and a printed script (no slide tray). If a casette narrative is desired, add $5.00 to the purchase price.

Please allow a month for delivery and specify, if possible, several rental dates to choose from.

Q. Has anyone made a good film about the bluebird and if so, where can I procure a copy of the film?

A. There is an excellent 20 minute film entitled "Bluebirds - Bring Them Back", which is available for rent or purchase from Berlet Films, 1646 Kimmel Road, Jackson, MI 49201. Purchase price of the film is $345. Video casettes may be purchased for $230. Either the film or the casette may be renter for $35. We can personally speak of the excellent quality of the film, both as to content and presentation. It was previewed at the 6th International meeting of NABS and was quite well received. By Walter and Myrna Berlet.

Q. I read in SIALIA sometime back that an open bluebird house seemed to promise some sucess in being accepted by bluebirds but not by House Sparrows. What is the result of these experiments?

A. Yes, this was being tried on several bluebird trails. These were regular bluebird houses with part of the top cut away, whether circular or in a square, with hardware cloth attached over the cut away. A second type was similar but had an extension above the house proper to allow cross ventilation but eliminate some of the rain entering. The thought was that bluebirds did not seem to mind the rain but the House Sparrow did - thus making this type of house a deterrent to the sparrow. We have tried both types of open top houses on a trail in central Mississippi over a five year period with no takers, bluebirds or sparrows. Too, we have not heard that this proposal proved to be successful.

Q. Is there a minimum diameter for the conical or square guard to prevent a snake from reaching the bluebird house?

A. I can speak from my own experience with a conical guard and a rat snake crossing it to reach my Purple Martin colony of twelve gourds, mounted on six cross arms at the top of a two inch diameter fiberglass pole, thirty feet above the ground. I have had a full compliment of martins each year and thought I was protected by a twenty four inch diameter conical guard placed about three feet below the lowest cross-arm of gourds. One day during the peak of the nesting season I neither saw nor heard the martins. I could not understand what had happened. The second day I still neither saw nor heard a single bird. I was determined to keep a close vigil throughout the second day in hope of finding an answer. Just before dark I saw a head stick out of one of the top gourds. I watched. Was it a martin, or what? The head came out further and revealed itself as belonging to a snake. The snake climbed from the gourd up to the crossarm, glided over the crossarm to the gourd on the opposite side, about thirty inches away, and began entering that gourd, with part of its body still in the first gourd. It was looking for more birds and had eaten eggs, birds, and all the young, some each evening perhaps, until it had eaten the entire colony. Upon letting the whole gourd cluster down, we found no evidence of eggs, young martins, or adults. The snake was a rat snake about forty-six inches long and had restricted himself to the size of the gourd each day, coming out at night to have a feast until all was gone. So, now I am recommending nothing less than a thirty-six inch diameter conical guard, hoping that will be sufficient to prevent a crossover. Upon further investigation I have learned that a snake does not need to wrap itself around the tree, pole, limb or vine, but can climb vertically.

Q. I have been told about your Jackson Bluebird Project in Mississippi but I live in Louisiana.

How can I get bluebird boxes for a bluebird trail?

A. Since ours is a non-profit project venture, we cannot add shipping costs and time to our prices of ten houses for thirty-five dollars. However, we have people from Alabama, Tennessee, and Louisiana who buy our houses regularly. Perhaps your best solution is to plan ahead and find someone who is making a trip to Jackson during the year who will agree to pick up your houses. If it is one or two only that you want, we suggest that you order them from the North American Bluebird Society. Their rates are reasonable and they will ship. Also, you can be assured that the houses meet the recommended dimensions for bluebird houses.

Q. Our club has given thought to promoting the bluebird cause in our geographic area. Is there a television commercial available to help with this?

A. Yes, the North American Bluebird Society has a thirty second public service announcement (PSA) TV commercial promoting bluebird conservation. Copies of this tape are available for loan to members. Write Richard J. Dolesh, 17800 Croom Road, Brandywine, Maryland 20613. Enclose a check for $2.50 to cover postage, mailer and handling.

Q. Do earwigs cause bluebirds any harm?

A They should pose no problem. Spraying the box with a pyrethrin spray or dusting it with rotenone should provide temporary control.

Q. Do bluebirds change mates during a nesting season?

A. Usually they do not. However, sometime they do after an unsuccessful nest occurrence. This changing of mates does not occur usually during the course of a nesting cycle, though. The experience related so well by Tina Dew about "Mr. and Mrs. Blue" is a rare one, but most interesting.

Q. How important are drain holes and ventilation holes for bluebird houses?

A. Very important. The bottom of the house should have the four corners cut off to produce triangular drains at each corner. Also, the bottom should be recessed about one-half inch above the level of the four side bottom edges to prevent rotting of the wood from prevailing rain water accumulation. The box we recommend, for which plans have been show, has the best type of ventilation, opposite side openings across the top of the two side pieces under the roof of the box. This permits a much cooler house than closed side boxes with holes for ventilation. Also, it permits the bluebird landlord to observe any wasp nests attached to the ceiling of the box inside before opening the box.

Q. Can you suggest geographical areas that clubs or organizations might use to locate bluebird houses?

A. Yes, there are three that we think of for excellent possibilities. One is the cemetery site. What better, more calm and peaceful, unmolested location can be found? Particularly is this true of the many rural cemetery sites with excellent fences surrounding the area, ideal for locating bluebird houses. Another site is the golf course. We have several golf courses in the Jackson area that have placed houses on poles at each of the greens. Golfers delight in seeing bluebirds while playing. Also, in Ohio especially, the ever present mail box post has been found to offer an excellent place to locate a bluebird house. Boxes placed on the opposite side from the mail box opening have been found to attract bluebirds. The birds don't mind the daily mail delivery. There are other advantages, too, in using such a location. First, the post is already there, the area beneath the post is kept clear of grasses, weeds, and vines, and there are usually power lines overhead for the bluebirds to light upon.

Q. Can you suggest a bluebird project for our garden club that does not involve erecting bluebird houses? Our club is in the city but we are interested in helping bring bluebirds back.

A. Yes, we certainly can. One valuable contribution that your club could make would be to place copies of books about bluebirds in all of the city libraries. Another contribution would be to place a slide set about bluebirds in the libraries or own it yourselves and offer to put on slide shows in the city elementary schools and at the libraries. Still another suggestion is to visit your local newspaper editor and ask him to have a story written and released through his paper about the bluebird cause.

Q. I live in the Mississippi River Delta and haven't seen any bluebirds here. Is there any need for me to put up a bluebird house?

A. The wide, open space of the Delta, usually found in vast acreages of cotton and soy beans does not lend itself readily to bluebird attraction. However, some have found with surprise and great joy that bluebirds have shown up at properly located nesting boxes, even in areas where they have not been seen for years. In the spring bluebirds often search far and wide for a place to build a nest. This may take several years or it may occur soon after putting up the boxes - but it is well worth trying. Just keep the sparrow out of the boxes, if you can. This will help. Keep the boxes up for several years; some traveling bluebirds may finally see them.

Q. I have been told that bluebirds will not build near the sea coast because of the salt water. Is this true?

A. No, it is not true. Some of the best bluebird trails are found along the coastal areas. Of course, there must be fresh water in the vicinity, but it is hardly conceivable that adequate fresh water would not be found everywhere along our coastal areas. You can always add a bird bath, too, and keep it filled with fresh water.

Q. How often do bluebirds lay infertile eggs?

A. This is hard to determine. Infertility is a rarity more that a normal occurrence. I can speak of a case that occurred on one of my bluebird trails. A pair of bluebirds had infertility of all their eggs in the same box each year. This has gone on for four years in the same box. Every time the incubation goes beyond the usual time span, I have cleaned out the nest and eggs, only to have the couple try and try again. I am convinced that it is the same couple, for it is always the same box - though I have no positive proof. It is a sad experience, indeed, to find a pair trying so hard to raise young siblings with no success.

Q. I have read that the cowbird does not build a nest but lays its eggs in an active nest of another bird. Is this true of the bluebird nest? And how great a problem is it?

A. The cowbird poses no great problem to the bluebirds, for it rarely uses the bluebird house nest in which to lay its eggs. Some cases have been reported in the literature, but they are unusual cases. You will have no problem about cowbird usage of bluebird nests, very likely.

Q. Will the location of a bluebird box near a concentration of honey bee hives pose a problem?

A. Reports have been found that the location of bluebird houses near a large concentration of honey bee hives could discourage bluebirds from building in the houses. I have not found this to be true with bluebird houses located in the vicinity of only a few bee hives, but it would not seem advisable to locate bluebird houses in the vicinity of a large concentration of bees.

Q. Can you recommend some especially good magazines about bluebirds and bird watching?

A. There are many fine bird magazines, but I consider the following to be near the top of the list for lay people.

We recommend the magazine published quarterly by the North American Bluebird Society, *SIALIA* (Latin for bluebird). It has no equal for news coverage about the bluebird but has also added interesting articles about cavity nesting species. Too, it is definitely the journal for the layman, not full of technical terminology, but very practical. Write NABS, Box 6295, Silver Spring, Maryland 20906-0295.

Another excellent magazine is *AUDUBON*, a bi-monthly journal of the National Audubon Society, issued to its members and covering a wide field of conservation. This organization, through its local chapters, carries on extensive work in the field of ornithology and widespread wildlife conservation as well as environmental. Write National Audubon Society, 950 Third Avenue, New York City, New York 10022 for membership information and the address of the nearest chapter to your location.

The *BIRD WATCHER'S DIGEST* is an informative bi-monthly journal of general birding information. It is an excellent magazine for the layman and is rapidly emerging as one of the leading bird journals. Its articles are short and "meaty" and often are written by leading national figures in the bird world. Roger Tory Peterson has a regular column in the magazine, as do other nationally known birders. Write *Bird Watcher's Digest*, P.O. Box 110, Marietta, Ohio 45750.

BIRDING is the bi-monthly journal of the American Birding Association. This is the only worldwide organization for birders. If you enjoy bird watching, the American Birding Association may be just what you've been looking for. *Reader's Digest* referred to birding as a "sport for all seasons" and this journal will help all ages to enjoy it more. Write American Birding Association, P.O. Box 4335, Austin, Texas 78765.

Q. Have the Eastern, Mountain and Western Bluebirds been seen together very often?

A. This occurrence is not usually found. However, this can occur in geographical areas between the mountain regions of the Rockies and the Western and Eastern Bluebird territories. I can speak of an experience of my own in sighting all three species together. This was while vacationing at Queen Wilhemina State Park in northwestern Arkansas. There were four of us eating together in the dining hall when my eye was attracted to a couple of bluebirds outside resting on a telephone pole bracing wire. I immediately used the binoculars and the scene revealed one to be a Mountain Bluebird and one to be an Eastern Bluebird. After the meal, we went outside for a closer view and a gorgeous sight it was. We saw a Western Bluebird picking up bugs just below the site, hopping from the tree to the ground and back. All four of our party observed this occurrence, Rare indeed!

Q. Is it true that predators like opossums and raccoons will follow a human's trail scent from house to house as he monitors his boxes?

A. In areas where predation by raccoons and opossums is a problem, particularly the raccoons, bluebird landlords have found this to be true. They, too, have found that the problem can be partially solved by diverting their approach from house to house on each trip. Instead of walking directly from house to house down the fence row, walk back to the road (if that is possible) and down the road to the next house. Any new plan of approach will help to confuse the predator.

Q. Is there a person or group that I can write to for bluebird information about the Western Bluebird?

A. Of course there is always the *SIALIA* magazine to which you can write. We also can recommend writing to a very active group, the Portland Audubon Society, 5151 N.W. Cornell Road, Portland, Oregon 97210. Also, one of their members, Hubert Prescott, 13505 S.E. River Road, Portland, Oregon 97222, is a leading

authority on the Western and Mountain Bluebirds.

Q. I travel from my rural home into the city every
day, about twenty-five miles each way, and
have observed bluebirds sitting upon the power
lines along the road, wishing that I could entice
them over to my place. Is there anything I can
do about this?

A. We know of no way that you can entice those
bluebirds to fly over to your domicile, but we can
give you a tip on what you might do for those
particular bluebirds. This comes from a nesting
box report on bluebirds by a landlord in Terry,
Mississippi, who had reported an unusual
number of bluebirds fledging for the year on his
reporting card to the Jackson Bluebird Project;
so much so that I was inclined to call him to find
out the secret of his success. He told me that he
had made himself a bluebird trail along the
highway from Terry to Jackson. Each day, to
and from Jackson he would observe the power
wires and when he saw a pair of bluebirds
together on the wire, he would make a note of
the exact location and on the return trip the
next day he would place a bluebird box in the
immediate vicinity of the viewed pair. He later
started carrying boxes in the trunk of his car
and by leaving home a bit earlier he could stop
and put up the house as he saw the pair on the
wires. He stated that this was the way he had

been able to report such success with bluebirds.

Q. Do bluebirds migrate and if so, from where to where?

A. Yes, bluebirds do migrate; however, they have no well established pattern for this like most migrating species do. Bluebirds are known to migrate south as the weather in winter threatens, but many times only sufficiently far to get beyond the inclement weather. Often their judgment is inadequate and many perish, particularly if the weather becomes much more severe and quickly so. A very severe, long spell of cold weather may push them to the southern states and some into Central America. So, there is not a standard pattern. Some will not migrate, even in very cold weather and often survive the cold weather. Bluebirds tend to group together for feeding and protection during the winter months; so, we see them in twenty or thirty, or even larger groups across their range.

Q. How long do bluebirds live?

A. There seems to be no way of determining the exact logevity of any bird species. All we have to go on is the latest longevity recorded in the United States Department of the Interior, Fish and Wildlife Service, Office of Migratory Bird Management. These records are determined from bird bands submitted voluntarily by persons who send in bird bands that have been recovered from birds for various reasons. So, from their records as of this year the longevity of the Eastern Bluebird is eight years and zero months.

It is possible, they state, that the banders may have a retrap that is older, since the department does not process retraps to the same area.

WHERE TO GET SUPPLIES

Audubon Workshop, 1501 Paddock Drive, Northbrook, Illinois 60062

Autumn Innovations, Inc., Drawer 18426, Greensboro, North Carolina 27419

Backyard Birds & Co., 717 S. Broadview, Springfield, Missouri 65804

The Barn Owl, 2509 Lakeshore Drive, Fernville, Michigan 49408

The Bird Feeders Society, P.O. Box 243, Mystic, Connecticut 06355

The Bird's Nest, 7 Patten Road, Bedford, New Hampshire 03102

Bird Specialty Products, P.O. Box 852, Kenosha, Wisconsin 53141

The Crow's Nest Book Shop, Cornell Laboratory of Ornithology, Sapsucker Woods Road, Ithaca, New York 14850

Duncraft, Wild Bird Specialists, 25 S. Main Street, Pennacook, New Hampshire 03301

Hyde Bird Feeders, Hyde's of Waltham, 56 Felton Street, Waltham, Massachusetts 02154

Lydia's Audubon Shoppe, 394 Washington Street, Bay Saint Louis, Mississippi 39502

Make Tracks, 3253 Warrick - F, Royal Oak, Michigan 48072

North American Bluebird Society, Box 6295, Silver Spring, Maryland 20906-0295

The Nature Store, 59800 S. Highway 97, Bend, Oregon 97702

Wild Birds Unlimited, 1430 Broad Ripple Avenue, Indianapolis, Indiana 46220

The Wood Thrush Shop, 3825 Bedford Avenue, Nashville, Tennessee 37215

Wood World Creations, Box 134, North Attleford, Maine 02760

Your own local Seed and Feed and Yard and Garden Shops.

Other Popular Items Available from Nature Books Publishers

THE BLUEBIRD - by Lawrence Zeleny

BLUEBIRDS SEVEN - by Bruce Horsfall

CHIMNEY SWIFTS AND THEIR RELATIVES - by Margaret Whittemore

PLANS FOR A 12-PLEX ALUMINUM PURPLE MARTIN HOUSE

THE PURPLE MARTIN - by R.B. Layton

THIRTY BIRDS THAT WILL BUILD IN BIRD HOUSES - by R.B. Layton

TEN PLANS FOR BUILDING PURPLE MARTIN HOUSES

Write for latest flyer on description and prices of available books

Nature Books Publishers

P.O. Box 12157

Jackson, Mississippi 39236-2157

(601) 956-5686

BIBLIOGRAPHY
(annotated)

Barrington, Rupert. 1972. A Garden for Your Birds. New York: Grossett and Dunlap.
This book shows how every garden, no matter how small or unpromising, can be turned into a sanctuary for many kinds of wild birds and not just tough old regulars like sparrows and starlings. It tells how you can help the birds in your area to breed and flourish, not only by feeding them in bad weather but also by providing them with nesting sites, artificial and natural, and by seeing to it that they are left unmolested by their natural and human enemies.

Bent, Arthur Cleveland. 1968. Life Histories of North American Birds. Washington: Smithsonian Institution Press (United States Natural Science Museum), Dover Publications reprint.
This is the most complete study of North American birds that is available, a basic resource set for all naturalists and ornithologists.

Blakeley, Lou and Jenks, Randolph. 1984. Birds at a Glance. New York: Van Nostrand Reinhold Company.
This offers a system of identification based on the **little** you see when you glimpse that elusive bird.

Cruickshank, Allen D. and Helen. 1958. 1001 Questions Asked About Birds. New York: Dover Publications reprint, 1976.
Sections on migration, breeding, growth, ecology, etc. An excellent quick reference piece for your library.

Darling, Lois and Louise. 1962. Bird. Boston: Houghton Mifflin.
A book for bird watchers who wish to go beyond the identification stage. A presentation of scientific writings with clarity and vividness for which the non-specialist will be grateful.

Dennis, John V. 1985. A Complete Guide to Bird Feeding. New York: Alfred A. Knopf.

This book is a complete treatise on bird feeding. It answers most of the questions that usually arise about feeding our avian population. Well illustrated and excellent photographs.

_____. 1981. Beyond the Bird Feeder.. New York: Alfred A. Knopf.

Written especially for those who feed birds, Dennis focuses on the birds' habits during the peak feeding months and explains some of the things they do when they are around the feeders as well as out of sight.

Dorman, Caroline. 1969. Bird Lore. Baton Rouge, Louisiana: Claitor's Press, Publishing Division.

A well spun story series by a lifetime birder who learned the secrets through her intimate terms with the birds on her 120 acre tract of forest, pond, and running streams of Louisiana.

Harrison, George H. 1976. Roger Peterson's Dozen Birding Hotspots. New York: Simon and Schuster.

Describes in detail the twelve best places in North America for seeing the most spectacular array of birds and bird behavior. The text is supplemented by beautiful photographs and a special section follows each chapter with tips on what to take; where to stay; how far ahead to plan and where to write for information; availability of groceries, gas, campsites, and restaurants.

_____. 1979. The Backyard Bird Watcher. New York: Simon and Schuster.

This book is a must for any beginner wishing to start birdwatching. The author leads you through feeding stations, housing, water, handling of pets, caring for the injured, and an outstanding chapter on photography.

_____. 1981. America's Favorite Backyard Birds. New York: Simon and Schuster.

A chapter on each of America's most popular songbirds, a look at their mating, nest life, food needs, enemies, longevity. This book is written for those who love birds and want to know more about them.

Harrison, Hal H. 1984. Wood Warblers World. New York: Simon and Schuster.
Comprehensive life histories of the 58 species of wood warblers that nest in the United States and Canada.

———— 1975. Field Guide to Bird's Nests. New York: Houghton Mifflin Company.
An often overlooked book but a great help in identification of birds by their nests and eggs. Excellent photographs, in color, of nests and eggs, with drawings of each bird and a narrative about each.

Horsfall, R. Bruce. 1978. Bluebirds Seven. Portland, Oregon: Audubon Society of Portland.
The history of this book is similar to that of another book about nature by Edith Holdins, The Country Diary of an Edwardian Lady, a surprise best seller. This is a charming book ostensibly for children, but the art of this well known nature artist deserves attention from everyone who appreciates birds and nature art. It is a very special book for children, since it covers the life of young bluebirds.

Hines, Bob and Peter A. Anastasi, 1973. Fifty Birds of Town and city. Washington: United States Department of the Interior.
A concise, one page description of each with illustration in color. A quick, ready reference for a most concise summary.

Imhoff, Thomas. 1976. Alabama Birds. Tuscaloosa, Alabama: University of Alabama Press.
Describes 378 species found in Alabama, 365 birds in color. Serves for the southern states as well and most birds for every state. A very complete treatise.

Krutch, Joseph Wood and Paul S. Erickson. 1962. A Treasury of Bird Lore. New York: Paul S. Erickson, Inc.
A rich compilation of writings for every taste, written by almost every significant naturalist of the day since Mark Catsby. There are five parts: Flight (13 authors), Family Matters (14 authors), Birds of a Feather (24 authors), Birds and Men (24 authors), Extinction and Conservation (9 authors). This is your chance to have narrative stories by over 80 authors.

Laycock, George. 1976. The Bird Watcher's Bible. New York: Doubleday and Company.
Contains information on attracting birds to your feeding stations, how to find and identify birds, bird photography, song recordings, bird watching sites in the different states, with 205 photos.

Layton, R.B. 1969. The Purple Martin. Jackson, Mississippi; Nature Books Publishers.
This is the only book on the species that is endorsed by national and international ornithologists. It is a complete and authentic guide to one of America's favorite birds. Well illustrated with photographs and drawings.

_____. 1977. Thirty Birds That Will Build in Bird Houses. Jackson, Mississippi, Nature Books Publishers.
Describing thirty birds which can be attracted to man-made houses, with photographs of each, photographs of their eggs, graphs of their songs, suggested plans and drawings for their houses, summer nesting range maps, silhouettes for comparison, and other worthwhile information.

Lentz and Young. 1985. Birdwatching-A Guide for Beginners. Santa Barbara, California Press.
An excellent guide for the beginning birder.

Lowery, George H. 1974. Louisiana Birds. Baton Rouge, Louisiana: LSU Press.
Describes 411 species of birds that have been observed in Louisiana: generously illustrated, with a discussion on each bird. Serves for other southern states as well and most birds for any state. This is a very complete treatise of the bird life of the 411 birds.

Parker, Bertha Morris. 1964. Baby Birds. Racine, Wisconsin: Golden Press.
This is a 25 page paperback activity book of Natural Science Series, well done and quite entertaining for the "wee" one, the early beginning birder.

Peterson, Roger Tory. 1980. A Field Guide to the Birds East of the Rockies. Houghton Mifflin Company.
This is the revised copy of Peterson's guide book and is the most used guide book in print, perhaps. Well done.

Quesada, Esther and Robert. 1984.
Has successfully captured on film the utterly fascinating day-to-day activities of our North American Species.

Reilly, Edgar M. 1968. The Audubon Illustrated Handbook of American Birds. New York: McGraw Hill.
While not a handbook to be carried about in the pocket, it is a comprehensive, informative, thorough, and definite description of the habits, life history, and appearance of every bird in the United States - nearly 875 species. It is "the book to which we turn when we want some item of information about a species or group of species, stated precisely, with brevity, and above all, authority", notes Dr. Olin Pettingill, Jr., the editor in chief, in his foreword.

Robbins, Chandler S., Bertle Bruun and Herbert Zim. 1983. Birds of North America. New York: Golden Press.
A concise one volume book for all North American birds. A favorite field guide among the birders. It is our recommendation for the most useful of field guides.

Schultz, Walter E. 1983. How to Attract, House, and Feed Birds. New York: Collier Books.
The most complete and easy to follow guide of its kind. It tells you all you need to know about providing food and shelter for birds, to help these wildlife creatures to survive.

Scofield, Michael. 1978. Bird Watching. Marshall, California: The Great Outdoors Trading Company.
This book is designed to be a basic access tool for the sport of birding. It gives people wishing to get started, all the information they need, and gives experienced birders a a complete reference guide for getting the maximum out of their field trips.

Shantz, Bryan R. and Pearman, Myrna D. 1984. Nest Boxes for Alberta Birds. Red Deer, Alberta, Canada: Ellis Bird Farm LTD.
This forty-two page, 8½ x 11, booklet in beautiful color is "intended to increase public participation in the conservation of native cavity nesting birds and to collect and publish information on the nesting ecology of those species in Alberta". It contains information on thirty-one species of cavity nesting birds which are found in Alberta.

Simonds, Calvin. 1984. Private Lives of Garden Birds. Emerson, Pennsylvania: Rodale Press.
About the lives of ten familiar birds found in the gardens and backyards of North America.

Weber, William J. 1982. Attracting Birds and Other Wildlife To Your Yard. New York: Holt, Rinehold and Winston. (Van Nostrand Rinehold Company).
With concern and love for all forms of wildlife, Dr. Weber tells how to choose plants and trees that will be beneficial to birds and small mammals. He discusses artificial feeding, and tells how to attract the greatest diversity of birds by using various kinds of seeds, as well as suet and peanut butter cakes. There are chapters on feeders, water and waterers, and bird houses, and information on how you can help the beautiful Eastern Bluebird or lure the tiny hummingbird to your yard using special feeders filled with sugar syrup. In short, with the help that Dr. Weber offers, you can formulate your own plan for attracting wildlife, feathered or furry.

Zeleny, Lawrence. 1976. The Bluebird. Bloomington, Indiana: The Indiana University Press.
This is the leading authority on the bluebirds. Written by one who has spent a lifetime in the study.

INDEX